The Inspiring Teacher

New Beginnings for the 21st Century

ROBERT A. SULLO

The Inspiring Teacher

New Beginnings for the 21st Century

ROBERT A. SULLO

The Inspired Classroom Series

NEA PROFESSIONAL LIBRARY

ADVISORY PANEL

Rosalind Lucille Yee
Reading Specialist
Prince George's County School System
Annapolis, Maryland

Arlene Lewis Dykes
Third Grade Teacher
Disnard Elementary School
Claremont, New Hampshire

Melissa W. Earnest
Teacher
Caldwell County High School
Princeton, Kentucky

James Duggins
Professor of Education
San Francisco State University
San Francisco, California

Thomas Ousley
Director of Attendance
Jennings School District
Jennings, Missouri

Copyright © 1999 National Education Association of the United States

Printing History
  First Printing: June 1999

This book is printed on acid-free paper.   This book is printed with soy ink.

ACID FREE
∞

Library of Congress Cataloging-in-Publication Data

Sullo, Robert A., 1951-
    The inspiring teacher: new beginnings for the 21st century /
Robert A. Sullo.
        p.   cm.— (The inspired classroom series)
    ISBN 0-8106-2955-0
    1. Teaching. 2. Effective teaching. I. Title. II. Series.
LB1025.3.S85 1999
371.102—dc21   99-30484 CIP

This book is for my parents, Blase and Evelyn Sullo.
Every child should be so lucky.

Contents

Acknowledgements

Like virtually every student who has experienced some success, I have been helped by many inspiring teachers. I'm sure I have unintentionally omitted some, but I want to acknowledge the following very special people: my parents, Mrs. Cronin (Weymouth Public Schools), Miss Mahoney (Weymouth Public Schools), Mr. Lewis (Weymouth Public Schools), Mr. Emerson (Weymouth Public Schools), Mr. Dwyer (Weymouth Public Schools), Dr. Callahan (Holy Cross College), Dr. Savage (Boston College), Dr. Kelly (Boston College), Dr. Glasser (The William Glasser Institute), and Eric Jensen.

Thanks, too, to all of my colleagues in the field of education, both those with whom I have worked during the past twenty-five years in the Plymouth Public Schools in Plymouth, Massachusetts, and those whom I've encountered in training workshops across the country. Your willingness to share stories and experiences has helped me become a more competent educator.

Finally, I wish to thank my wife Laurie and our three children (Kristy, Greg, and Melanie) for their unwavering support and help in all I do.

Introduction

Teaching is the noblest profession. I don't intend any disrespect toward other fields, nor am I suggesting that critically important contributions aren't made in any number of professions. Still, in a democratic society, teaching offers a nobility that eludes other pursuits. Teachers have the joyful task of helping young minds discover one of the most important lessons in life: that learning to the best of our ability—using the capacity of our amazing brains—enriches us in countless ways. Inspiring teachers teach much more than facts and subject matter. They teach a way of being in the world. They help students discover the joy of becoming lifelong learners.

In an address on September 2, 1997, to the membership of my local association in Massachusetts, President Jane Russell said, "Teaching is the profession that makes all other professions possible." It's not an exaggeration to say that the future is in the hands of our teachers. In so many other fields, professionals know what they have before them. There is less mystery about what the future may hold. In classrooms every day, teachers face unlimited potential. Each classroom is filled with students who may grow into leaders in their professions or less well-known but valuable contributors to their communities.

Each teacher has the potential to inspire the next great scientist, musician, entrepreneur, artist, scholar, author, entertainer, doctor, or teacher.

It's hard to imagine how any teacher could not be passionate about teaching every day. We have the capacity to create environments that will encourage greatness in our students. That opportunity deserves to be called "awesome," and it explains why teaching is the noblest of all professions.

I'm delighted that you have decided to explore what it takes to become an inspiring teacher. If you are willing to make the commitment, you will live a life with richness that can never be measured in dollars. No material accounting system can quantify the value of having inspired even a single child, let alone many.

ABOUT THIS BOOK

The Inspiring Teacher draws on my personal experience and the collective wisdom of the teachers I've worked with over the years. It discusses the key issues facing those who wish to become inspiring teachers.

I've been a public educator since 1974. During that time, I've held positions as an English teacher, a school psychologist, and an adjustment counselor and worked with prekindergarten children through high school young adults. Since 1988, as a faculty member of the William Glasser Institute, I've presented workshops about choice theory and quality schools.

My workshops have given me the opportunity to meet thousands of teachers from around the country. I've shared many ideas and strategies with them, and in turn I've learned an enormous amount. They've told me what works well for them. They've told me of their struggles. I've met beginning teachers who possess great energy and enthusiasm. I've had the pleasure of working with veteran teachers who are just as energetic and inspired because they know that the work they do every day with their students matters tremendously.

If you have a passion for learning and a love of children,

you have the potential to become an inspiring teacher. Those two ingredients alone, however, are not enough. You need to know about human motivation and how to manage people effectively. You need valid information about how people learn most easily and efficiently. You need to be familiar with child development and be able to appreciate what is expected from children at various stages. You need to know how to work well with colleagues. You need to know how to engage parents and create positive alliances with them that will help inspire their children. You need the skills to help people resolve conflicts effectively and respectfully. You need to develop strategies that will allow you to make the most of your valuable time. You need to be committed to changing what you do and how you do it as new information and new technology change what we know about the best practices in education.

This book will provide a solid foundation as you strive to become an inspiring teacher. It is not, however, meant to be an exhaustive work. Many of the topics deserve to be rigorously explored through further reading, workshops, or courses. In addition, certain elements that are critical to good teaching are beyond the scope of this book. The bibliography lists some books and Web sites that will help you begin learning more about the topics introduced here.

The Inspiring Teacher is written primarily for three related audiences. One audience is those who are in the process of becoming teachers or who are exploring whether teaching is the profession for them. Another is those who are just beginning their careers—new teachers who have a desire to inspire the students in their classes. The third audience is experienced teachers who want to rekindle their joy in teaching. It is easy for teachers to get so caught up in the routine of teaching that they slowly lose some of their enthusiasm. By combining their wisdom with a fresh energy, such teachers can revitalize their classrooms and take an even greater pleasure in their profession than they did in the earlier years.

HOW THIS BOOK IS ORGANIZED

This book is divided into two parts: foundation and application. Part I provides an overview of choice theory, brain-based learning, and important developmental issues. Familiarity with the concepts presented in this section will enable you to take full advantage of the strategies offered later in the book. Part II helps you move from knowledge to application. It discusses how you can apply the concepts from Part I to inspire students and colleagues and build positive alliances with parents. It also contains chapters on conflict management and time management.

A SPECIAL GIFT

The word education comes from the Latin *educare*, "to draw out." The word inspire is derived from the Latin *inspirare*, "to breathe into." *The Inspiring Teacher* will help you breathe life into students by drawing out their potential. It's an arduous task, but its pursuit is worthwhile because inspiring teachers possess a special nobility and experience a joy that makes their lives truly special.

As you begin this book, take a moment to reflect upon those special teachers who inspired you. You may have met them in elementary school, graduate school, or somewhere in between. They may have been academic teachers, coaches, advisers, counselors, or administrators. You may have known of their special gift to you when they gave it, or you may not have realized until years later how inspirational they had been and how much they had contributed to your growth and development. They may be available for you to thank today, or they may be gone. Regardless, take a moment to give all of them the heartfelt thanks they deserve. Then recognize that you too can give the same gift to your students in the years to come. You can become an inspiring teacher.

PART I

Foundation

CHAPTER 1

The Qualities of an Inspiring Teacher

No recipe offers directions for becoming an inspiring teacher. Since individuality is one of the essential attributes of an inspiring teacher, there is no way to provide a single definitive list of characteristics that such a person would embody. Still, nearly all gifted teachers share certain qualities.

ABILITY TO DEVELOP POSITIVE RELATIONSHIPS

The most important element in becoming an inspiring teacher is the ability to develop positive relationships with others. Teaching is steeped in interaction, and successful teachers know how to relate to others in mutually satisfying ways. The most obvious relationship is between teacher and student. Successful teachers are also able to forge positive collaborative relationships with colleagues and parents. Chapters 5, 6, and 7 discuss these relationships in detail.

Inspiration is nurtured in relationship. If you know your

subject matter well but don't relate well to students, you will only be successful with highly motivated students. Other students may do enough to get by. You may even develop sufficiently rigorous standards that most of your students will learn a great deal. But you will never inspire them. Inspiring teachers understand that positive relationships with students serve as the foundation for successful teaching and learning. They dedicate as much energy to building strong relationships as they do to developing strong learning plans.

Think about teachers who have inspired you. Almost certainly there was a special relationship between you and them. They communicated that they valued you, respected you, and were there to help you. They expected you to do your best. You never doubted that they had your best interests in mind as they taught you. This kind of relationship has the capacity to inspire. It is the kind of relationship that every student deserves.

Creating relationships that have the capacity to inspire is not easy, commonsense work. Students will often behave in intentionally or unintentionally hurtful ways. They won't always appreciate the value of what you are trying to teach, and they may do less than their best work. They'll sometimes behave in a way that suggests disinterest or boredom. They may even be overtly hostile and defiant. Common sense would suggest that you move away from students when they display negative behavior. If you take that approach, you may be able to manage reasonably well. You will almost certainly survive. But you'll forfeit your opportunity to inspire disconnected students and unleash their positive potential.

A commonsense approach yields common results. If you think enough students are regularly doing quality work, then common sense and the status quo will suffice. I believe that many more students are capable of producing quality work but have yet to be inspired to do so. The way to inspire these students is by forging positive relationships with them.

Students should always be treated with respect and dignity, even when they behave in unacceptable ways. One of our central roles as educators is to help students grow academically and learn more effective, responsible, respectful ways to behave. We are less likely to be drawn into counterproductive behavior if we stay focused on our role instead of being sidetracked by students' inappropriate behavior. If we lose our focus, we can easily become demeaning, moralistic, sarcastic, and angry. None of those behaviors helps us do our jobs better. Maintaining a respectful approach with students is always preferable.

Early in my first year as a ninth-grade English teacher, an incident occurred that illustrates the importance of positive relationships. I was giving my first spelling test and one of my students, Tammy, was obviously copying from her neighbor's paper. I moved near her table, but she didn't stop. I quietly asked Tammy to move her seat. She asked me why. I simply repeated my request. Quite unexpectedly, Tammy got up, kicked her chair over, yelled, "Well, *#*# you!" and stormed out of the room.

Following her suspension, Tammy, a bright student, did reasonably well, at least in terms of her grades. At that point in my career, I didn't understand the importance of relationship very well. Tammy had hurt and humiliated me. Common sense led me to interact with her as little as possible. We both survived, but I never inspired her.

Today, I would handle the situation differently. I would work hard to find a way to engage Tammy. I would make it clear to her that as offensive as her behavior had been, I was still there to help her be successful. I would not allow her to abuse me, but neither would I allow her abuse to keep me from reaching out to her. I would not be controlled by her poorly developed coping strategies. I would offer to help her grow.

When I reflect upon my eight years as a classroom teacher, I know that I was reasonably successful because I had the ability to relate positively with most of my students. Without compromising my authority in the classroom, I made it clear to students that I liked them. We laughed a lot in my classroom. We enjoyed each other. I don't believe I was as technically skilled as many of my colleagues, but I was successful because I forged positive relationships with my students. We were partners in the quest to become more educated and more skilled. Although I had occasional problems with student behavior, I usually handled them with relative ease because the students and I genuinely liked each other. In a setting with positive working relationships, students have little motivation to be disruptive. Significant learning is almost certain, and inspiration remains a possibility.

PASSION FOR LEARNING

Inspiring teachers have a passion for learning. They soak up the richness that life offers them. They are excited by each new morsel of knowledge they acquire and each new skill they develop and apply. Many are synthesizers, pulling together seemingly disparate concepts and weaving them into a meaningful whole.

The passion for learning is not restricted to educational and academic pursuits. Inspiring teachers recognize that there is always more to experience, and that each new experience enriches them and makes them even more valuable resources for their students. A passion for learning may express itself in traditional book learning, the earning of advanced degrees, and the development of special curricular expertise. It may also express itself in an enthusiasm for travel. Visiting places and cultures that some have only read about helps the inspiring teacher turn a mundane classroom experience into the spectacular. A passion for learning may express itself in the development of particular hobbies. Special interests—learning for the sake of learning and enjoyment—can serve as a wonderful way to introduce students to the pleasure that comes with the in-depth exploration of a topic.

LIFELONG LEARNERS

Being a lifelong learner is part of having a passion for learning. Regardless of their credentials, inspiring teachers never finish learning. They are always on the journey.

Inspiring teachers often put themselves in situations where they are unskilled and unknowledgeable, creating the opportunity to reexperience the challenge, excitement, and fun of being a new learner. A master teacher once told me that she intentionally set out to have at least one significant learning experience every year. The substance of the new learning was unimportant. Her goals were to connect with the feeling of ignorance that comes with any new learning, to learn to value that feeling rather than fear it, and to be open to new ways of thinking and being. Another inspiring teacher I know continues to bask in new learning in his retirement years. It's a delight to listen as he talks with excitement, energy, and enthusiasm about his discoveries.

ACTIONS MATCH WORDS

While I was conducting a workshop some time ago, a poster in the room caught my attention: "If we don't model what we teach, we are teaching something else." Inspiring teachers model what they teach. Students young and old know whether teachers are genuine by observing their classroom behavior. Congruence is respected and fraudulence is always unmasked. The tyrannical teacher who teaches the value of democratic principles can never hope to inspire. The writing teacher who is never seen with pen in hand or fingers on the keyboard will have a harder time convincing students that writing is an enjoyable and worthwhile pastime.

You are always modeling whether you want to or not. Students will pay close attention to your actions. Does what you say you advocate match what you do? As long as your words and actions match, you have the capacity to inspire.

LOVE AND APPRECIATION OF CHILDREN

If you want to become an inspiring teacher, it is imperative that you love and appreciate children. A love of your subject matter is helpful but insufficient. In fact, if you love your subject more than you love children, you will never be able to inspire. You will be wonderfully successful with those who already value your subject, but that is good teaching, not inspiring teaching. To inspire students who may be unaware of why your subject is important, you must first demonstrate that you care for them.

There are no perfect relationships, and there will be times when you may not enjoy your students. To have those moments occasionally is normal. If you find yourself disliking large numbers of students and complaining about students in general, you probably are in the wrong profession. It's true that teachers today face more challenges than their predecessors did. It's equally true that students today can be inspired to produce quality work and to take pride in doing their best. When kids act like kids and you find yourself smiling, you're on the right track. While you don't encourage disruptive behavior, you accept that sometimes students will be disruptive. Your love and appreciation of children in such circumstances never diminishes.

OTHER QUALITIES OF INSPIRING TEACHERS

When I conduct workshops, I often begin by asking the teachers to identify the qualities they would like to see in me. Since all students want to be inspired—including teachers in professional workshops—the comments represent qualities that I believe are helpful to those seeking to become inspiring teachers. Each workshop is different, of course, but teachers consistently mention the following qualities. The inspiring teacher will:

- be open minded.

- facilitate a learning environment in which all students

feel valued and believe they can make important contributions to the group.

- provide concrete strategies and model what is to be accomplished.
- communicate an enthusiasm for the subject matter.
- help students understand that learning will be worth the effort.
- display a sense of humor, making sure it is always respectful, not hurtful.
- demonstrate a deep knowledge of the subject matter.
- be flexible and allow students to achieve course objectives in various ways.
- respect students unconditionally.

Doing all the right things does not guarantee success. Teachers can still fail to inspire if they also engage in counterproductive behaviors. Following is a list of some things that inspiring teachers should not do. The inspiring teacher will not:

- repeat ideas beyond the point of usefulness.
- talk in a monotone and teach lethargically.
- talk "at" or "down to" students.
- belittle or berate students.
- seek to gain approval from the group at the expense of a student.
- disengage from the students.
- ask students to accept responsibility for their behavior while refusing to accept responsibility for his.
- ask students to do something that she would not do or would not want her own child to do.

THE THEORETICAL FOUNDATION

Even if you already possess many or all of the qualities discussed in this chapter, you will find it beneficial to have some additional knowledge and skills as you strive to become an inspiring teacher. In the next three chapters, you will have an opportunity to explore three areas that I believe are critically important for educators in the 21st century: choice theory, brain-based learning, and child development.

A description of choice theory provides you with a model for understanding behavior and taking positive advantage of the internal motivation that resides within each one of us. An introduction to brain-based learning offers you some specific ideas about how we learn most easily and efficiently, along with some practical suggestions to help you develop a learning environment that will foster quality academic work. Finally, a discussion of some fundamental child-development concepts helps you differentiate between appropriate behaviors and behaviors that should be cause for concern. These three chapters will equip you with the foundation necessary to put the ideas presented in this book into practice.

SUMMARY

All inspiring teachers are unique. They bring such different gifts to their classrooms that they are almost impossible to categorize. Despite their many differences in style and temperament, however, most inspiring teachers possess a core set of qualities. More than anything else, inspiring teachers know how to develop positive relationships with their students. They communicate to their students that they expect quality work and that they will help students achieve both academically and socially. Inspiring teachers have a passion for learning. They demonstrate through their actions that they are lifelong learners, always open to new, enriching learning experiences. In addition, what inspiring teachers "practice what they preach," which is one of the reasons why students have such respect for these special teachers.

Inspiring teachers bring energy and enthusiasm into their classrooms, and they expect their students to work hard. They establish environments where learning is a joyful, never-ending journey of discovery. Inspiring teachers respect students, never belittling them or speaking sarcastically in the classroom. Finally, inspiring teachers build their teaching strategies on a solid understanding of human behavior, motivation, brain-based learning, and child development. By combining personal qualities, knowledge, and skill, they create classrooms in which both students and teachers thrive.

CHAPTER 2

Choice Theory

Effective teaching largely depends on an understanding of human motivation. Without this knowledge and the ability to apply it well, few teachers can be inspiring.

Various theories provide an explanation of motivation. The most prevalent theory in our society and elsewhere in the world is external control psychology. Derived primarily from the work of John Watson and B.F. Skinner, external control psychology can be summed up as follows: human behavior is a response to outside stimuli. When people are rewarded or reinforced for a particular behavior, they are more likely to engage in that behavior again. Conversely, when people are punished for a particular behavior, they are less likely to engage in it again.

External control psychology is attractive to many. First, it is a wonderfully simple, "commonsense" explanation of behavior and motivation. It takes incredibly complex and multifaceted human beings and reduces them to simple reactive entities capable of being controlled by applying rewards and punishments. Second, external control psychology appeals to those who seek to control. It posits that our fellow humans are easily manipulated once we develop an effective system of rewards and punishments. With that knowledge, we can shape the behavior of others the way we wish.

Despite its prevalence, external control psychology is fundamentally flawed and can never be effectively applied by anyone who hopes to inspire quality. We are much more complex than external control psychology would have us believe. We are not simple reactive creatures capable of being programmed like robots. In fact, because we have a drive to be autonomous, any attempt, however well intentioned, to shape our behavior will always be met with defiance. Put simply, people do not accept being shaped, even when it is apparently for their own good.

Can the ideas of external control psychology ever be used effectively? Yes, if the goal is compliance rather than quality. If all we care about is simple compliance, approaches based on external control psychology might work reasonably well. For example, if I want you to perform a simple task, one without gradations of quality, I might be able to use the principles of external control psychology. Under these specific conditions, I might be able to entice you with a reward or create sufficient fear with the threat of punishment to get you to do what I desire.

In education we generally don't look for simple compliance. We seek the best work a student can produce. As long as we rely on approaches that are based on a belief in external control, we are destined to be no more successful than we have been until now. In short, external control psychology has taken us as far as it can. It is a psychology whose applications can coerce into compliance but never inspire toward quality.

Let's look at the use of an external control approach for homework, an area frequently devoid of quality. Students are often rewarded with check marks for completing homework. They are punished with low grades and a loss of credit when they don't do their homework. On the surface, this strategy seems reasonable. Examine what often happens, however, under these conditions. Students "complete" the homework, receive the reward, and perhaps even gain recognition with celebrations like "homework heroes" for having "done" all the assigned homework. Relying on the principles of external control psychology, we have many compliant students. Unfortunately, the completed home-work is not necessarily quality work. In fact, teachers commonly give full credit for work that is horrifyingly inadequate simply because it has been done. Are you satisfied with this result? Would you rather learn how to inspire?

Choice theory is a relatively new theory of behavior and motivation developed by William Glasser (1998). Choice theory provides a way of understanding human beings that is respectful of the complexity of what it means to be human. It can be applied in any situation involving human interaction. I believe that all who hope to become inspiring teachers owe it to themselves to become familiar with choice theory. A thorough understanding of this psychology will help you work more effectively with students, parents, and colleagues. It will provide you with the skills to inspire quality work by many more of your students.

Choice theory differs from external control psychology in several ways:

- **Internal motivation.** External control psychology suggests that we are externally motivated by rewards and punishments. Choice theory maintains that we are internally motivated. The outside world can only provide us with information. It does not make us *do* anything. This perspective doesn't mean that outside information is irrelevant or unimportant. Still, as active—not reactive—beings, we are internally driven and choose our behavior.

- **Personal responsibility.** Choice theory leads to a belief that we are responsible for our behavioral choices. External control psychology suggests that we are "shaped" by external stimuli. If that view of human behavior is true, then being held accountable for our actions is fundamentally unfair. We are simply the products of an endless stream of rewards and punishments that have been placed upon us by our parents, teachers, and society.

- **Free will.** Choice theory teaches us that we have free will. In fact, it proposes that one of the drives built into our genetic structure is the drive toward freedom and autonomy. External control psychology suggests that freedom is an illusion. No less a major figure than Skinner said as much. Practitioners of external control psychology have a view of humanity that denies free will. Choice theorists, in contrast, view human beings as exercising free will every day.

It is beyond the scope of this book to provide a complete overview of choice theory. Three components essential to inspiring quality student work are presented here. They focus on our universal basic needs, the source of motivation, and the way we develop our perceptions of reality.

BASIC NEEDS: GENETIC INSTRUCTIONS AFFECTING BEHAVIOR

We are all born with genetic instructions. There is little argument that we have been given genetic instructions for physical characteristics such as height, eye color, and the shape of the nose. Choice theory proposes that we have also been given a set of five genetic instructions that affect our behavior: to love and be connected to others, to seek personal power and competence, to be free and autonomous, to be playful and have fun, and to survive. The first four of these genetic instructions are psychological. The need to survive is physiological. Throughout our lives, all our behavior is purposeful. That is, we each act in ways designed to help us follow the instructions built into our own genetic structure.

The genetic instructions, also called the basic needs, are universal. It doesn't matter if you are young or old, male or female, rich or poor. Typically, the basic needs are discussed in a given order—love and belonging, power, freedom, fun, and survival—but no ranking or hierarchy is implied. If there is a hierarchy, it exists at an individual level, not at a general level. Just as some of us are tall and some short, for example, the genetic instructions that affect our behavior vary from person to person. Some people are highly social (love and belonging). Others are energized by each new challenge and are always seeking ways to become more skilled (power and competence). Still others are driven by a need for autonomy (freedom), sometimes at great cost, or are always in pursuit of joy and play (fun). Finally, we all are acquainted with people who would never skydive, bungee jump, play the stock market, or engage in any high-risk behaviors (survival).

The need for fun is not any less important or serious than the other needs. Choice theory teaches us that fun is intimately connected to learning. For that reason, fun is especially important in education. It is not coincidental that the most inspiring, educationally rich classrooms are fun-filled for students and teachers alike.

While the basic needs for some people may be present in various intensities, they may be more equally balanced in others. No one need is preferable or less desirable. The basic needs do not motivate us directly anyway. The quality world does.

THE QUALITY WORLD

Our basic needs are drives to behave. For example, we are driven to be loving and connected to others, but we are given no preset notion about how to be loving or where to direct our loving behaviors. The same is true for the other basic needs. Nature has given us the drive, or "tendency toward," not the specifics. Over time, we develop specific perceptions of those people, things, behaviors, and ideals that are the most need-satisfying and important to us. This special place in our minds, called the quality world in choice theory, represents our individuality. Everything in our quality world is connected to one or more of the basic needs. While all of us are driven by the same basic needs, each person's quality world pictures are necessarily different from another's. My quality world, for example, includes my family, my most cherished beliefs and values, and those behaviors that are most need-satisfying to me.

When choice theory says that we are internally motivated, it is referring to the quality world pictures that reflect our individuality. We are motivated by the things and people in our quality worlds. To determine whether something or someone is in your quality world, ask yourself these questions: How hard would I work for this person or thing? Would I be willing to endure pain and hardship on behalf of this person or thing? Put simply, we work hard for what is in our quality worlds. Motivation is the willingness to work hard to achieve something internally desired or valued.

A word of caution: What we put into our quality worlds is not always good for us. Things become part of our quality worlds because they are need-satisfying, not necessarily because they are a responsible or positive choice. A student may put behaving disruptively into his quality world because it helps him satisfy the needs for power and freedom. While that choice is understandable, it is certainly nothing we wish to endorse or encourage.

How do we handle this issue? It is wise to remember the following three central principles of choice theory:

1. All behavior is purposeful.

2. All of us are doing the best we can.

3. People have the capacity to do good. No one sets out to do otherwise.

With these three notions in mind, we have a way to understand and manage troublesome quality world pictures. Since all behavior is purposeful, it makes sense from a particular point of view. When we are confronted with behavior that we don't fully understand, we might be inclined to identify it as "crazy." Once we do so, we forfeit our ability to work successfully with the person who engages in that behavior. It is much more helpful to understand that the goal of all behavior is to satisfy the basic needs built into a person's genetic structure.

It is also helpful to remain mindful that all of us are doing the best we can to satisfy our needs. This principle does not mean that we operate at our potential every moment. It does mean that any behavior represents our best attempt at a specific point in time to get what we want, even though we might think of something different several days, minutes, or seconds later. This principle does not excuse irresponsible behavior or suggest that we encourage people to do less than they are capable of doing.

The third principle—everyone has the capacity to do good, and no one sets out to do otherwise—is especially helpful when we are dealing with troublesome behavior. If we remember it, we maintain our focus: to help students learn responsible ways to satisfy the needs built into their genetic structures. This perspective helps us be effective teachers. Many students in today's classrooms seem intent on disrupting the education process. Some even intentionally behave in horribly violent ways. Our best chance to manage these students successfully is to remember that they have the capacity to behave responsibly. The goal of an inspiring teacher is to help students learn how to satisfy their needs without turning to antisocial behavior.

Teachers usually know which of their students are most at risk for acting out violent behavior. To minimize the chance of violence erupting in their schools, teachers directly address this issue by doing the best they can to engage and include *all* of their students. Given recent events, many schools are finding it worthwhile for staff to meet and collectively brainstorm ways to engage students in responsible behaviors and help them feel part of the greater school community.

The power of the quality world to direct our lives cannot be overstated. Once something is in our quality world, it has tremendous energy and is very motivating. We seek to live in ways that mirror what is in our quality worlds. The inspiring teacher does everything possible to help students construct socially positive, quality world pictures and to develop the requisite responsible behaviors to bring these pictures to fruition.

External Control Versus Internal Motivation

I attended a meeting some years ago about a student, Tim, who was not doing well in school. Earlier, the parents had requested an evaluation to determine whether Tim had a learning disability or some other special education need that would explain his school failure. Testing had revealed that he had average cognitive ability and no indications of any learning disability.

We were discussing ways to help Tim be more successful. An area of special concern was his failure to do homework. One person suggested that Tim earn a point each time he completed a homework assignment. Tim would earn the point regardless of how well he did the homework. Since Tim loved and excelled in hockey, his parents would link playing hockey with the number of points he earned. If he earned enough points, he could play hockey. If he didn't, he would not be allowed to play.

Everyone at the meeting had Tim's best interest in mind. Everyone except me believed in a commonsense, external control approach. I believed that the proposal was horribly anti-educational and something no inspiring teacher would ever want to do. We would be teaching Tim—through actions, not words—that doing homework is nothing more than a means to something worthwhile (in his case, hockey). Any action that diminishes the value of learning has no place in the repertoire of the inspiring teacher.

How might we have better worked with Tim? Using the concepts of choice theory, we would have begun by respecting Tim's quality world pictures at that time. Instead of making playing hockey contingent upon completing homework, we would have examined two areas. First, we would have discussed with Tim why he valued hockey. As we showed genuine interest in something he enjoyed, he would have seen us as allies—adults interested in him and what he cared for, not simply adults who wanted him to conform to their expectations. Discussing hockey with Tim would also have given us a glimpse of his most important basic needs. Such information would have been useful in structuring a need-satisfying school experience for Tim. We then would have worked with Tim to help him appreciate that completing his homework, working to the best of his ability, and fully involving himself in the process of education are worth doing. They are not worth doing in order to play hockey. They are simply worth doing for their own sake.

Second, we would have looked at the system rather than the symptom. By focusing our energy on trying to "fix" Tim by helping him earn points so that he could play hockey, we missed the opportunity to do something potentially more significant. What is it about homework that leads some students to ignore it completely or do it with little pride and energy? It is simplistic and erroneous to say that students who don't do homework are "lazy" or "unmotivated." When Tim played hockey, for example, he was not lazy or unmotivated. Such labels are misleading.

School Activities That Satisfy Basic Needs

Is hockey—or any other activity—inherently more valuable and worthy of students' attention and effort than schoolwork? I don't believe so. We can always find students who care nothing at all about activities such as hockey.

All students can put working hard on schoolwork into their quality worlds. Educators would be wise to take a close look at those activities where students consistently work hard and see what factors are present. Countless so-called lazy, unmotivated students, for example, work as hard as anyone else in the areas of athletics, drama, and music. What variables link these activities?

First, these activities easily allow students to follow the basic need to belong. Even in a sport involving individual competition, such as tennis, players are still part of a team and the sense of belonging is need-satisfying. Students who take part in music or drama activities feel a similar sense of belonging that is sufficiently motivating to get them to long, often arduous practices and to work hard while there.

Second, these activities give students a sense of personal power and competence. In competitive athletics, losing is a part of the terrain, but skilled coaches help young athletes feel a sense of accomplishment even if they don't win. Athletes still want to win, sometimes fiercely, but winning isn't the only way to feel a sense of power and competence. Coaches help athletes value developing and improving skills. Drama and music performances similarly help students experience power and competence in a healthy, responsible way. Young musicians facing a difficult piece of music, for example, work incredibly hard to develop competence because it feels good to work hard and be successful.

Third, students satisfy the need for freedom in extracurricular activities precisely because they are electives. Participating in something voluntarily changes the experience dramatically for many.

Fourth, athletics, drama, and music generally involve a high degree of fun and learning. Of course, they also involve a lot of hard work. Some coaches are even considered to be tyrants. But more often than not, these are joyful experiences for students and coaches alike. Coaches generally have no need to be tyrants because team members have the activity and doing well firmly in their quality worlds. They willingly do what coaches ask to the best of their ability.

Athletics, drama, and music are all highly need-satisfying. Give students something need-satisfying to do, and they will be highly motivated and do their best almost always. As choice theory maintains, all our behavior is purposeful, and the purpose of all our behavior is to satisfy the basic needs built into our genetic structures. If you ask people to do something that is not satisfying to them, they will probably either defy you or perform only well enough to get you to leave them alone. On the other hand, if you ask them to do something inherently need-satisfying, they will do what you ask with energy and enthusiasm.

Not every activity we offer our students has to satisfy multiple needs to be successful. If we structure our classrooms with the concepts of choice theory in mind, however, students will produce significantly more quality work in a much more joyful atmosphere.

Creating a Need-Satisfying Environment

To inspire successfully, we need to structure classrooms that are need-satisfying. Can you give students opportunities to interact appropriately, taking advantage of the basic need for belonging? Can you offer them academic challenges that satisfy the drive for power and competence? Such activities should not be so overwhelming that students believe even their best efforts will result in failure. While teachers may worry that creating challenging activities for different skill levels is impossible, remember what happens in athletics, drama, and music. Those activities bring together students with different skill levels. Still, all are challenged to achieve to the best of their ability, allowing them to feel a legitimate sense of power and competence. The same approach could be applied in the academic classroom setting.

In most secondary schools today—and probably for years to come—certain courses are required. Some may believe that having required courses means it is impossible to cultivate an environment compatible with the drive toward freedom. I disagree. Creating an environment that recognizes the need for freedom does not necessarily mean that people do what they want when they want. Many systems, schools included, require that certain things be done at certain times or in a certain way. Still, within any given structure, we can seek ways to provide options so that the need for freedom is accommodated. For example, during Black History Month, my educational goal might be to have students appreciate African-American history and the political and social complexity of present-day race relations. There are a number of ways for this goal to be achieved. For example, students may choose to stage a debate, put on a theatrical, create a multimedia report prepare an investigative news report, or work with other classes on a school-wide project. Any or all of these projects provide a way for students to achieve the learning outcome developed by the teacher.

Any inspiring classroom will be characterized by fun. The inspiring teacher intentionally seeks a way to build a sense of joy into the learning plans. To do anything else would be foolish. Can you imagine ever inspiring anyone in a joyless environment? Students might learn some content, but in such an environment no one would be inspired to pursue more learning.

Teachers around the country who are familiar with choice theory are intentionally creating need-satisfying classrooms. They consistently report that their students do quality work more regularly than before. Have students changed? I don't think so. The conditions in which students are being invited to learn have changed. In a need-satisfying environment, students and teachers flourish.

Let's return to Tim, the student who would not do his homework. In approaching his situation from a choice theory perspective, we would have looked at how need-satisfying the homework assignments were. Too many of us assign homework that is of little value and expect it to be done simply because we have assigned it. If the homework truly has value, we should help students appreciate that fact. Otherwise, homework may be perceived negatively and may not be done well, assuming it gets done at all. If we help students see the value of what we are inviting them to do, we will see a dramatic improvement in the quality of their work. With Tim, our emphasis would have been to build a positive relationship with him and help him put working hard in his classes and doing homework into his quality world.

Understanding the quality world and the central role it plays in motivation is essential if we hope to create inspiring classrooms. When we talk about "internal motivation," we are referring to the quality world. When we put learning into our quality worlds, we produce our best work. We profit from feedback and coaching, and there is never any question about our motivation and willingness to work hard.

Most teachers I have met say that they would love their jobs more if they could face classrooms of motivated, eager learners. Class size is an important issue. Another important consideration is students' inherent cognitive abilities. But these and other factors become almost incidental in relation to motivation. Give a good teacher a room full of motivated, eager students, and wonderful things happen, regardless of class size and the inherent cognitive abilities of the learners. Give the same teacher a small group of highly intelligent youngsters who have no desire to learn what is being taught, and the job becomes a nightmare. When you understand choice theory and can help more students put learning what you are trying to teach into their quality worlds, you will be on your way to becoming an inspiring teacher.

Gaining Credibility with Students

If you are attempting to help your students put something new into their quality worlds, you need to be credible. They will wonder why they should listen to you. The way you present yourself, your subject matter, and your values is important in determining whether most students find you credible enough to affect their quality worlds. It is essential that you are perceived as genuine. If students sense that you are a fraud, they will naturally shut you out. Once that happens, little you say will make a difference. Conversely, when students believe that you genuinely care about them, want them to be as successful as possible, and will always help them achieve as much as possible, they will generally work hard.

Two people may each have something valuable to tell students. One may be heard and the other not. To effectively provide valuable information, teachers have to demonstrate to their students that they care about them. The saying that captures this idea is "They have to know that you care before they care what you know."

PERCEPTION

Our perception of reality determines how we will act. According to choice theory, information from the outside world passes through three filters before it becomes a perception in a person's brain.

First, the sensory filter receives information. Until we sense something, it essentially doesn't exist for us. The sensory filter can distort incoming information to some degree. A common example is when we act according to what we heard—what our sense of hearing told us was true—and later discover that we heard inaccurately.

A second filter through which information passes is called the total knowledge filter. Human beings are natural meaning makers. We attempt to make sense of the world and all incoming information. As new information reaches us, it is screened against everything we already know, the total knowledge filter. Information may exist in some "pure" form in the real world, but it is altered as it passes through the total knowledge filter. We interpret incoming information on the basis of our previous knowledge, regardless of how complete or accurate it is.

The information in this chapter provides a good example of how the total knowledge filter contributes to the development of any perception. Some of you have previous knowledge about choice theory. Others are encountering this information for the first time. Although the printed words are the same for all readers, each of you brings your past experience and knowledge to the process of reading and develops different perceptions according to what is in your total knowledge filter.

The same process operates within any classroom. Suppose you are providing some direct instruction about early America as part of a whole group activity. Students' perceptions may vary considerably because of their distinct total knowledge filters. A student who has been to a living history museum will perceive your discussion differently from a student who has not had that experience.

Sometimes teachers want to help others change their perceptions. For example, some students may seem content with mediocre academic performance, apparently oblivious to the consequences. One way to affect the perceptions of others is to provide them with additional information. By adding to their total knowledge filters, their perceptions necessarily change. Remember, however, that for people to be receptive to information you want to share, you usually need to have enough of a positive relationship with them that they are willing to let the information in for consideration.

The third filter is called the valuing filter. We are evaluative creatures. We need to be in order to survive and thrive. All of us—even those who strive to be nonjudgmental— evaluate every bit of information we encounter. We ascribe a positive, negative, or neutral value to all incoming information using the following standard: Is this information need-satisfying?

The valuing filter proposed by choice theory is supported by scientific inquiry. Brain researcher Pierce Howard (1994, 150) writes: "Today a consensus is emerging that embraces the notion that events with the potential to elicit emotional response must first pass through the appraisal activity of the mind.... Researchers agree that it takes place between stimulus and response. When we receive 'news' from our environment, it is neither good nor bad until our appraisal process has passed judgment." Howard's "appraisal activity" and "appraisal process" are equivalent to the valuing filter.

In prehistoric times, when many more of us were primarily concerned about survival, the valuing filter served to inform us whether incoming information was a threat. Today, the valuing filter also concerns itself with our psychological needs. When we see someone we care about, for example, we ascribe a highly positive value to that person. When we see someone who has been disrespectful to us, we ascribe a negative value to that person.

We are not objective about the information we receive. If we have a negative feeling about someone or something, it significantly affects how we interpret any accompanying information. An extreme example will make this clear. Suppose I am an alcoholic. If you and I have either a neutral or negative relationship and you try to help me see that my behavior is leading me toward disaster, I will probably perceive your well-meaning attempt to help me as meddlesome and will reject the attempt. Without my conscious intent, my valuing filter will affect my perception in such a way that I do not benefit from your important information. On the other hand, if you and I have a highly positive relationship, I will perceive your comments differently. What you tell me may be difficult to hear and involve substantial pain. I will probably, however, be more receptive to the information because I have a perception that you care about me and that you are a need-satisfying person to me.

The same process happens every day in every classroom. The valuing filter affects how teachers perceive students and how students perceive teachers. To make sure students are open to our information, we need to work on helping them perceive us as need-satisfying. When they value us, they profit from the valuable information we have to offer. When they don't value us, they may reject our valuable information. The role of the valuing filter highlights the importance of developing positive relationships with students. Any professional educator who attempts to inspire quality without nurturing strong appropriate relationships with students is doomed to failure.

SUMMARY

Choice theory is a new way to look at human behavior and motivation. Unlike external control psychology, it affirms that we are active, creative beings who choose our behaviors because we are internally motivated. We are born with universal drives, basic needs built into our genetic structure. Our experiences lead us to develop highly individualized quality world pictures, the source of all internal motivation. We are willing to work hard for the things in our quality worlds because we believe they are need-satisfying. Our three filtering systems—the sensory filter, the total knowledge filter, and the valuing filter—affect how we construct meaning from the information we receive.

The inspiring teacher influences all three filtering systems by making sure students are paying attention (sensory filter), regularly providing students with more information and skills (total knowledge filter), and communicating caring and respect for the students (valuing filter). In this way, the inspiring teacher helps students put learning and working hard into their quality worlds. Appreciating the critical importance of positive relationships, the inspiring teacher intentionally behaves in ways that help students profit from whatever information they have been invited to consider. Finally, the inspiring teacher fosters an environment in which students are able to meet their basic needs by doing what the teacher asks. In such an environment, behavior problems are usually rare and more easily handled. Academic performance and a love of learning soar.

This chapter has provided an overview of some key elements of choice theory. To learn more, see the bibliography for suggested books and Web sites. The more knowledge you have and the more you can act in a way consistent with that knowledge, the more you can inspire students to do quality work in your classroom.

CHAPTER 3

Brain-Based Learning

All effective teaching is "brain compatible." To inspire quality in the classroom, teachers should have a basic knowledge of how the brain functions and the principles of brain-based learning. Brain-based learning is an approach to learning that is built on current research in neuroscience about how the brain learns most easily and efficiently. It is not tied to any one theoretical model.

Many successful teachers unintentionally create brain-compatible classrooms and learning plans. Through years of experience, they have developed classrooms where students are inspired and discover the joy inherent in working hard and learning as much as possible. While some have had the good fortune to stumble into wonderful teaching strategies, being intentional about how to teach effectively is one of the qualities of the inspiring teacher.

Brain-based learning is informed by a wide range of the latest research on the brain and learning, not by a specific well-defined theoretical framework. Although such research-driven information is important, I believe that it is also important to be guided by a single theory of human behavior. Being grounded in a single theory allows us to be consistent in how we understand the many behaviors we encounter in schools. Choice theory has proved to be a valid way to understand human behavior. Choice theory and brain-based learning are mutually supportive. The concepts presented by both choice theory and brain-based learning will enhance your performance in the classroom and enable you to move toward becoming an inspiring teacher.

This chapter reviews some of the major concepts of brain-based learning. Because new research and new ideas are being generated so rapidly, I will discuss only well-established brain-based information. I encourage readers to become familiar with current literature about learning and the brain. To learn more about brain-based learning, see the bibliography.

BRAIN INFORMATION FOR THE NONSPECIALIST

Many of us know virtually nothing about the brain. To gain a full understanding of brain-based learning concepts, every teacher should have some familiarity with the functioning of the brain, including basic brain anatomy.

The average brain weighs about three pounds and is composed of roughly 100 billion cells (Jensen 1996, 7). In comparison, a monkey has about 10 billion brain cells. However, it's not the number of brain cells that's important but the number of connections these cells can make. Researchers are uncertain about the number of possible connections that can be made within the human brain. Estimates range from 100 trillion possible connections to more than the number of atoms in the known universe (Jensen 1996, 7).

Comparisons between the brain and the computer are invalid. The abilities of the human brain far outstrip the most sophisticated computer. The brain is designed to be a multiprocessor. At any given time, it is processing color, movement, emotion, shape, intensity, sound, taste, and weight and also identifying and creating patterns and making meaning of incoming information (Jensen, 1996, 8). Researchers now believe that the slow, linear approach used in many classrooms inhibits learning because the brain lacks enough stimulation. Most brains thrive in an environment with significantly more input. Interestingly, because a rich, multifaceted environment is so much more brain friendly, students are considerably more engaged, and discipline problems are dramatically reduced.

Left and Right Hemispheres

The brain is divided into two hemispheres. It was once believed that each hemisphere controlled different functions. In fact, both hemispheres are involved in nearly every behavior, certainly all complex behaviors.

A band of fibers known as the corpus callosum is critically important in helping the two hemispheres communicate with each other. While there are other points of interhemispheric communication, the corpus callosum is the single most important area. If the two hemispheres were not able to communicate, information sent to the right hemisphere would be unavailable to the left hemisphere and vice versa.

Even though the whole brain is involved in virtually every complex behavior, each hemisphere does have primary responsibility for particular functions. Having certain areas of the brain specialize leads to greater efficiency. In most people, the left hemisphere is more involved in processing language. It is more analytical and sequential. The right hemisphere tends to appreciate the whole and is the more visual hemisphere. The left hemisphere tends to be more linear in its reasoning and concrete in its orientation. The right hemisphere appreciates randomness and looks for relationships instead of seeing bits of information in relative isolation.

That said, hemispheric preference is not an absolute. Music, for example, is generally associated with the right hemisphere. Researchers have found, however, that professional musicians process music much more in the left hemisphere. Apparently, their expertise in the field leads them to use the more analytical left hemisphere when processing music. Countless other examples refute the typical left-right tendency, so be careful not to assume that a particular activity is necessarily related to the left hemisphere or right hemisphere for every learner. Despite this caution, the inspiring teacher intentionally structures a learning environment that respects the processing style of each hemisphere and maximizes the chances of every student feeling engaged and connected. Be sure to include activities that reflect both a left-hemisphere orientation (sequencing tasks, literary activities, factual information, and a linear structure) and a right-hemisphere orientation (visual learning, open-ended questions, experiential learning, and moving from general to specific).

Communication Within the Brain

With 100 billion cells, the communication network within the human brain is vast and complex. Information being processed by the brain must pass from cell to cell. It moves from the cell body of a neuron, an impulse-conducting cell, through the neuron's axon. At the end of the axon is a small gap, the synapse, that separates two neurons. On the other side of the synapse is the dendrite of the neighboring neuron. The dendrite, the receptor site of the neuron, carries information to the cell body. The information then moves down another axon to the next synapse. Sufficient electrochemical energy is required for the neuron to "fire" and send the information across the synaptic gap. Neurons operate on an "all or none" principle: either there is sufficient energy for the information to traverse the synapse and arrive at the next neuron intact or there is insufficient energy and the transmission stops. The number of synapses that must be successfully negotiated in even the most routine behavior is astounding.

Critical in this process of neuronal communication are the neurotransmitters. They are stored within the neurons and are released provided there is sufficient energy. The neurotransmitters move into the synaptic gap, carrying the information from the axon of one neuron to the dendrite of the next. Once the transmission is complete, the neurotransmitters are reabsorbed by the original neuron.

More than 50 neurotransmitters have been identified. Some of the most commonly known are dopamine, glutamate, endorphin, norepinephrine, and serotonin. Our levels of neurotransmitters can significantly affect our perceptions, emotions, learning, and memory. Proper nutrition and exercise can help us maintain appropriate levels of neurotransmitters. Inspiring teachers, regardless of what they teach and the grade level of their students, may want to educate students about the critical importance of proper nutrition and exercise in building a more efficient brain.

CREATING THE BRAIN-COMPATIBLE LEARNING ENVIRONMENT

The inspiring teacher intentionally creates an environment where learning can flourish. Learning can be either conscious or nonconscious. Jensen (1996, 44) explains, "When we say [conscious learning], we mean that we are aware of what we are learning, while we are learning it. Nonconscious learning means acquisition—we are taking it in, but there is no attention or awareness of it. Most classroom learning happens without the knowledge of the teacher." While we may spend hours developing learning plans for our students, the vast majority of what they learn is acquired nonconsciously. "Dr. Emile Donchin, at the Champaign-Urbana campus of the University of Illinois,... says that more than 99% of all learning is non-conscious. Your students are learning without knowing it. They are constantly picking up learning from visual cues, sounds, experiences, aromas and other environmental cues that far exceed any content from a lesson plan or course" (Jensen 1995, 35).

Inspiring teachers take advantage of nonconscious learning. For example, the use of posters and other peripherals can enhance any learning environment. If you accept that your learners' attention will wander at times, doesn't it make sense for them to encounter things that support your goals? Choose posters and other peripherals for their potential value in teaching, not merely to create an "attractive" classroom appearance. Posters with inspirational quotations or tranquil scenes from nature help build a relaxing environment that promotes learning. Key course concepts and content can be prominently displayed so that learners nonconsciously encounter them even when they are seemingly "not paying attention." To maintain a learning environment that is novel and inviting, teachers should regularly change the visuals used in the classroom.

Student work can also enhance the learning environment. Inspiring teachers demonstrate that they value the work their learners produce by displaying samples around the room. Of course, to demonstrate the greatest respect, ask students to choose the work.

Music

Music is a powerfully effective peripheral. The September 1, 1994, edition of the NBC program Dateline explored the effect of music, specifically the music of Mozart, on learning. Researchers found that listening to selected compositions by Mozart during learning can measurably increase spatial learning, memory, and reasoning. Like the Dateline information, other research has found a connection between the brain and Mozart's music. In studies involving preschool, secondary school, and college students, computer-generated graphs of brain-wave activity look remarkably similar to Mozart's scores (Jensen 1995, 217).

Other studies confirm the positive relationship between certain music and learning. Research by a college entrance exam board discovered that those students who had studied music for four or more years scored higher in both verbal and math tests. Further, countries with the top science and math scores all have strong music and arts programs (Jensen 1995, 218). Steven Halpern (1985) writes, "Important new evidence shows that not only is the study of music beneficial in itself, but the introduction of [it] into a school's curriculum causes marked improvement in math, reading, and the sciences" (quoted in Jensen 1995, 219). Clearly, music is not a frill, something to be cut when budgets need to be trimmed. Music and the arts contribute significantly to traditional learning. We cut them at our peril.

Not all music has a positive impact on learning. Inspiring teachers should be judicious when using music in their classrooms. Relaxing music is the most effective in helping students settle down and focus (Halpern 1985, quoted in Jensen 1995, 220). One example is baroque music written in a major key. A benefit of using music during instructional times is that it doesn't matter if the students consciously hear the music or especially like it. Simply having it playing softly in the background will encourage a relaxed atmosphere conducive to learning.

It is probably best to play music that students do not know particularly well. When a familiar piece is heard, many of your learners will attend more to the music and less to the material you are presenting. Make sure that the music you use enhances the desired learning and does not unwittingly interfere with what you are trying to teach. You do not need to use music at all times. The best advice is for teachers to experiment and build their own library of effective classroom music.

Novelty and Ritual

Our brains are structured to attend to anything novel in the environment. Because novelty may represent danger, we give special attention to anything new. Instead of bogging down a classroom in too much routine, inspiring teachers intentionally build novelty into the learning environment. Each time teachers introduce a new concept, they create a novel situation. This strategy is effective for two reasons. First, the novelty leads the brain to attend more closely, maximizing on-the-spot learning. Second, the uniqueness of the presentation makes it easier to develop stronger memories. (I will say more about memory later.)

The brain also thrives on ritual. While there is undeniable value in novelty, there is also a degree of threat and stress. Ritual and predictability offer relief from stress and are equally beneficial to the brain. The inspiring teacher structures a classroom that has many rituals so that students know what to expect at certain times. One example of an effective ritual is the use of certain music. An inspiring teacher may find it helpful to have calm, soothing, brain-compatible music playing when the students enter the room. Another ritual many teachers use involves having a "problem of the day" for the students to work on as soon as they arrive. A brief journal-writing time at the beginning of each class is a common ritual.

Novelty and ritual are two sides of the same coin. The more ritual you incorporate, the more your learners can tolerate and profit from novelty. Too much novelty without sufficient ritual creates a stressful environment that inhibits learning. With adequate ritual and predictability in the environment, however, the brain invites increased novelty. This brain-compatible balance of novelty and ritual helps create an inspired classroom.

Providing Challenges and Feedback

Inspiring teachers are skilled in creating environments that enrich the brain. Two strategies will be outlined here: creating a challenging environment and providing learners with ample feedback.

The most appropriate learning environment is characterized by high challenge and low threat. An insufficiently challenging learning environment robs students of the opportunity to grow. Returning for a moment to the choice theory notion of power as a genetic instruction, we can see how this works. In an "all-nurturing" environment, expectations are low and students have limited opportunities to satisfy the need for power and competence by engaging in meaningful schoolwork. In a challenging classroom, however, students who successfully master complex tasks satisfy their need for power in a productive, socially positive way. Inspiring teachers invite students to tackle challenging work. At the same time, they support students as they struggle and grow.

Students also thrive in classrooms where teachers provide ample feedback. Advocates of brain-based learning and choice theory agree that quality feedback enhances learning. I want to distinguish between feedback and criticism. Feedback involves providing information to learners so they can more effectively self-evaluate and improve the quality of their performance. Feedback is nonevaluative.

Criticism clearly is evaluative. One of the limitations of criticism is that it interferes with the natural tendency to self-evaluate and strive toward improvement. When criticized, people often tend to justify their ineffective behaviors instead of concentrating their efforts on enhanced performance. When given quality feedback, however, they can better self-evaluate and take steps to improve.

Let's examine the importance of feedback and the difference between feedback and criticism. When a student turns in a piece of writing, it likely represents his best effort at that time, provided the teacher has structured the assignment effectively. Even though the writing represents the student's best effort, it can still be improved. If the student is not given specific quality feedback, however, there is little reason to believe that he can substantially improve his work independently. It is not enough to simply tell the student to improve his work. The student needs specific feedback that he does not perceive as criticism.

What distinguishes helpful feedback from well-meaning but unhelpful "constructive criticism"? Much of the difference lies in how communication with students is structured. Effective communication helps students perceive your comments positively and profit from the wisdom you have to offer. Otherwise, your wonderful ideas will fall on deaf ears.

I might say to students, "Are you interested in having people pay more attention to you and your ideas?" The students will likely say yes because of the universal desire to be listened to (power). I would then say, "In this class, one of the things we work on is how to write more effectively. The more effectively we write, the more people will listen to us and our ideas." Instead of telling the students that writing is something they "have" to do, I have helped them see that writing is something they "get" to do and that effective writing will lead to an increased sense of personal power. Once this happens, the students and I have a shared quality world vision, an essential step in creating an inspiring classroom.

Next, I tell the students that I have more knowledge, expertise, and ability in the area of writing than they do. I want them to see my feedback as helpful to them in their growth as writers. With that objective in mind, I might say, "I'm delighted that you want to become better writers because that's one of the things I can help you do. I've been working on writing for a long time, and I'm still trying to get better. I've had many more opportunities to practice than you have, so I'll be glad to help you. I have a question for you. When you write something and turn it in to me, would it be helpful to you if I told you what I especially liked and what areas need additional work?" Again, my goal is to forge a shared quality world picture where students perceive my comments as helpful feedback, not unhelpful "constructive criticism." By linking my feedback to their comment that they want to improve their writing, they will develop a different—and more helpful—perception of what my comments mean.

Finally, I might say, "If getting my comments and ideas is helpful to you, I'm glad to do it. But here's another question. In order for you to see what I've written, would it be most helpful if I made my comments using a color that stands out from what you use? If you write in blue or black ink, would you be able to locate my comments more easily if I used red ink?" What happens seems almost magical, but it is really just what occurs when inspiring teachers do their jobs effectively. Suddenly, students favorably perceive papers peppered with editorial comments in red ink. This perception leads students to use the teacher's information as helpful feedback, not ignore it as unhelpful criticism.

Feedback is essential for the brain to maximize its potential. Used ineffectively, it can deteriorate into destructive criticism and interfere with learning and the natural quest for knowledge. In the hands of the inspiring teacher, rich feedback can accelerate the learning process and foster an increased desire to become more academically skilled.

Emotion

Emotion is critically important in learning. Anyone who attempts to take emotion out of learning, to make it a purely objective, cognitive event, is operating contrary to what is suggested by advocates of both brain-based learning and choice theory.

According to choice theory, behavior has four components: acting, thinking, feeling, and physiology. The feeling, or emotional, component in learning is no less important than the thinking, or cognitive, component. Research by brain scientists has suggested the important role emotion plays in learning. Briefly, experiences with a strong emotional content are more likely to be stored efficiently and subject to easier recall. Experiences with little emotional content are stored much less efficiently. The inspiring teacher wants all information stored efficiently and accessible to the learners when they need it. In an inspiring classroom, you are likely to encounter many of the following in an attempt to add emotion to the learning experience: enthusiasm, drama, role plays, lively debates, hands-on learning experiences, guest experts, and laughter.

The Impact of Threat

While positive emotion can enhance learning, negative emotion significantly reduces learning. Any behavior that makes students feel threatened should be avoided. Remember that the primary purpose of the brain is to keep us alive. When we are threatened, we shift into a survival mode. Our energy is spent making sure that we survive the perceived threat. Blood, oxygen, and life-sustaining nutrients are sent to the large muscles, readying us for the well-known fight or flight behaviors designed to protect us. The result is a decreased blood flow to the brain. The frontal lobes of the brain are the first affected and the area of greatest compromise during times of stress and threat. The frontal lobes are most involved in long-term planning, higher-level thinking, and problem solving. A student who feels threatened is more likely to exercise less effective judgment, behave impulsively, and be unable to access effective problem-solving strategies.

When we speak of the impact of threat, it does not mean physical threat exclusively. Alan Rozanski (1988, 1005-12) has conducted research indicating that sarcasm, criticism, and put-downs increase abnormalities in heart rate. Further, these abnormalities were as significant and measurable as those from a heavy workout or pre-attack myocardial chest pains. The inspiring teacher makes certain that the classroom is a place free of threat, both physical and emotional.

Positive Learning States

Brain researchers define a state as "a distinct body mind moment composed of a specific chemical balance in the body" (Jensen 1996, 49). There are various states, some better for learning than others. The inspiring teacher is able to both read and manage states effectively to enhance learning.

Each state has its own set of behaviors. In a challenging, low-stress environment that provides ample feedback, students are more likely to be in states that optimize learning. While the state you desire may differ depending on what you want your students to do, the following states are generally appropriate for learning: curiosity, anticipation, suspense, challenge, and temporary confusion. The inspiring teacher's behavior elicits these desirable states, preparing the students to be fully engaged in the learning.

It is important to learn to read students' states. When you scan the classroom and sense that the students are bored and disengaged, you need to take action that will lead to a state change. As long as students are locked into a boredom state, for example, you will not be able to inspire them. Instead of plowing ahead, the inspiring teacher recognizes the counterproductive state and acts to help students move into a state more conducive to learning.

Until the state is changed, the behaviors you see will likely remain unchanged. For this reason, brain-based theorists often say that all behavior is "state dependent." If you wish to change the behavior, change the state. Students who are "misbehaving"—behaving in ways not sanctioned by the teacher—are in a specific state. As long as they remain in that state, they are locked into the limited number of behaviors that accompany it. Most of those behaviors are not welcome in school. The most effective way to deal with unwanted behaviors in school is to help students change states. Once they move out of the less desirable state and into one more appropriate for school success, their behavior will change dramatically, almost instantaneously.

Mihaly Csikszentmihalyi (1990) calls one highly

⸗

desirable learning state "flow." It occurs when the task is neither too challenging nor too easy. He writes, "Challenges that are greater than your skills, that's anxiety. When your skills exceed the challenges, that's boredom." That special place where skill level and challenge meet leads to the ideal state of flow. While there is no recipe to create flow, you are most likely to get there when you provide an exciting environment that uses cooperative learning teams, challenges learners to do their best, and minimizes stress, pressure, and unnecessary deadlines.

Paying Attention and Making Meaning

Teachers often want their students to be in a state best described as "paying attention." Remember, though, that there is a distinction between paying attention and learning. In fact, while paying attention is a necessary component of the learning process, it is equally important for students to turn their attention inward in order to participate fully in the process of learning.

For learners to receive information from the outside, they must be externally focused. As new content is being introduced, paying attention is helpful. True learning only occurs, however, when externally derived content is processed internally. If students only pay attention, they cannot make meaning for themselves, and the learning process is incomplete. Once information has been taken in, it is essential that students focus internally—not pay attention—to make meaning of what they have received.

It is impossible both to pay attention and to make meaning simultaneously. If you are fully attentive (external orientation), you can't fully make meaning of what you are attending to. If you are making meaning (internal orientation), you can't fully attend to what is being offered from the outside. Students who are too attentive often fail to make adequate meaning. They learn material in a rote, superficial way. Because they have not fully processed the material, it is never truly theirs to use creatively and in a way that requires higher-level engagement. Those who are busy making meaning when teachers want them to pay attention are at a disadvantage because they are doing so without adequate input.

Inspiring teachers want their learners' attention just long enough for them to begin making meaning for themselves. To facilitate the process of making meaning, you should help students appreciate the relevance of what they are studying, introduce it with sufficient emotion so that it will engage students and increase the likelihood of them placing it in long-term memory, and assist the brain's tendency to create patterns by highlighting distinguishing qualities and relating new learning experiences to prior learning.

Remember that making meaning is an internal process. Advocates of choice theory and brain-based learning agree that there is no meaning in any information until we create meaning. All the outside world can ever provide us with is information. By paying attention, we gain access to information. As we process that information, we give it meaning and make it real, relevant, and useful. Inspiring teachers offer students an opportunity to pay attention and to make meaning so that students can make what they have learned their very own.

Nutrition

Too many of us connect proper nutrition with our ability to participate in overtly physical activities like sports and forget that efficient thinking also requires a healthy diet. We can eat in ways that improve brain functioning.

Teachers do have some impact, however small, on the diets of their students. Teachers can share information, and they can develop parent newsletters. Even with little ability to significantly improve the diets of students, teachers can choose to eat in ways that will improve their own overall health and functioning. (Of course, anyone considering a change in diet should consult a physician.) At a certification course for brain-based learning, held June 24-29, 1996, in Boston, Eric Jensen offered some information about brain-friendly nutrition.

The following foods can help boost alertness and mental performance: eggs, fish, turkey, tofu, pork, chicken, and yogurt. Egg yolks and wheat germ can enhance memory. Folic acid, found in leafy green vegetables, beef liver, and beans, can reduce depression and boost learning performance. The trace mineral boron, found in broccoli, apples, pears, peaches, grapes, and nuts, improves mental activity. Brain specialists recommend drinking 8 to 12 glasses of water a day. (By encouraging students to drink water, even in class, you can make a difference in their lives. Students who lack adequate amounts of water often display symptoms commonly associated with attention deficit disorder or behavioral disorders. Many teachers have found that students who bring water to class improve their performance.) Foods rich in iron, such as dark-green vegetables, meat, and fish, can enhance attention, memory, and visual-motor coordination. Polyunsaturated fats, unlike saturated fats, lead to increased learning and memory. Finally, the brain runs most effectively when a person eats small snacks or meals five to nine times per day.

Other Factors Affecting the Learning Environment

Color affects learning. Your particular personality and your state at any given moment will influence how a color affects you. For example, if you are highly stressed, red may lead to more aggression. On the other hand, if you are relaxed, red may be especially engaging and inviting. The most tranquilizing color, according to researchers, is sky blue (Jensen 1995, 57). (While this color may seem like an attractive classroom option, remember that you don't want your students too calm!) In general, dark colors lower stress and increase feelings of serenity. Bright colors are riskier because they have the capacity not only to excite and energize but also to increase aggressive and nervous behaviors. Research suggests that the best colors to enhance learning are yellow, beige, and off-white.

Plants can be a beneficial addition to the learning environment. NASA scientists have determined that plants remove pollutants from their environment and charge it with increased oxygen. Research studies conducted by the Federal Clean Air Council found that plants not only raised oxygen levels but helped increase workers' productivity by 10 percent (Jensen 1995, 64).

Finally, aromas may affect learning. Research conducted at Rensselaer Polytechnic Institute in New York found that students developed more ambitious goals, took on greater challenges, and got along better with peers when exposed to certain aromas (Jensen 1995, 65). The aromas that appear to facilitate alertness include peppermint, basil, lemon, cinnamon, and rosemary. Lavender, chamomile, orange, and rose are helpful in calming and relaxing.

The environment where learning takes place can be structured in ways that facilitate increased productivity and enhance learning. Yes, there are factors that affect learning over which we have little or no control. The inspiring teacher, however, accepts this limiting reality while at the same time creating an environment that maximizes learning for everyone in the classroom.

MEMORY

Memory is a fundamental psychological process and a significant factor in learning. Many once believed that our memories are like taped recordings of events. In fact, we now know that memory is much more of a creative, reconstructive process. Daniel Schacter, a professor at Harvard Medical School, said at a presentation in Boston on June 20, 1997, "We are the intervening issue between the world and what we create in our memory." Memories are not encoded as a whole and neatly stored in one part of the brain. Instead, bits of information are stored in various parts of the brain. "Remembering" involves reconstructing a reality from fragments in a way that is at least partially creative and subjective.

In order to recall something, we need the cues provided by association. The more associations we create when we encounter new material, the easier it is to recall that material when we need it (Russell 1979, 100). This complex process is facilitated by the tendency of the brain to create multiple associations when presented with novel information. (Remember, the brain pays more attention to things that are new.)

Connected to the concept of associations is "context dependency." Something is more easily recalled when a person is in the same state and location as when the original learning took place. Inspiring teachers often recreate the original learning state when asking students to recall information. For example, if students were studying an aspect of the American Revolution while listening to a particular sonata by Mozart, the inspiring teacher may have the same music playing when conducting a review or some type of assessment. The music provides a nonconscious association and allows the students to have easier access to what was learned. Inspiring teachers also intentionally structure situations that are decidedly different from those where the original learning took place to determine whether learners are able to transfer information to different contexts and different states.

The more unique a learning experience is, the easier it is for the brain to create efficient associations and remember the material for later use. For those who are uncomfortable with gimmicks or tricks intended to enhance memory, it is helpful to remember that the brain naturally creates associations. Peter Russell (1979, 129) says, "It is not that mnemonics are cheating, but rather by not consciously using them, one is effectively hindering the learning process. The brain is, in the end, going to form associative connections whether you help it or not."

Our short-term memory generally lasts about 5 to 20 seconds. For information to be moved into long-term memory, we need to create some type of association. The inspiring teacher helps students efficiently create associations. Inefficiently stored information may be "known" but unavailable for use. The retrieval of information is as critical as the encoding of information. The more we create uniqueness with new learning, the more easily information will be retrieved. Encoding information without sufficient clarity and distinction is akin to giving all your computer files the same name. You might know the information is somewhere on the hard drive, but there's a good chance it will be a slow, difficult process to locate it when you need it.

While we often speak of memory in global terms, there are actually different types of memory. Semantic memory is our memory for speech and text. Of the various types of memory, semantic is the least reliable. When we ask students to remember facts from books or class lectures, we are tapping into semantic memory. While there is nothing wrong with this approach, it would be wise to remember that people with wonderful memories may not do particularly well on this task.

Episodic memory is memory by event or location, memory embedded within a given context. For example, you are in the kitchen and think, "I need to get my notebook from my bedroom for tonight's class." You walk to the bedroom, only to find that you can't remember why you're there! You know you're looking for something, but you have no idea what. In this circumstance, many of us retrace our steps. Once back in the kitchen, you suddenly remember, "Ah, yes. The notebook."

Inspiring teachers take advantage of this powerful memory system in the classroom. They may ask students to visualize the context in which learning took place. As students become skilled in this strategy designed to access episodic memory, they will discover that they are able to remember much more than they thought possible.

The memory we create from hands-on learning experiences is called procedural memory. Memories like these are stored in the body and are among the strongest of memories. Many adults have not ridden a bicycle for years, but they still can ride with relative ease because the skills needed to perform that task have been stored in the body. Inspiring teachers make use of this type of memory by making sure students are physically active and engaged with their learning. Students who have the chance to perform, to participate in an active and vigorous debate, or to physically create something will be much more likely to access those memories because the associations have been wired into their bodies.

Finally, reflexive memory refers to memory that is the result of considerable repetition or that has a particularly strong emotional component. For many of us, multiplication facts are remembered effortlessly because of the repetitive nature of drills. Events with a strong emotional component lead to the creation of deep associations and lasting memories. Most people who were at least 10 years old have vivid memories of what they were doing and where they were on November 22, 1963, when they heard that President Kennedy had been shot.

Each memory pathway—semantic, episodic, procedural, and reflexive—is separate. Even though we may have stored information using multiple systems, our memory of any event or learning experience will be limited by the specific pathways we can access. When we are assessing student learning, we may ask questions that activate one memory pathway—for example, semantic—but not others. The resulting information we get may not adequately represent what students have learned. The inspiring teacher does everything possible to activate as many memory pathways as possible so that students are able to demonstrate their full knowledge.

GARDNER'S THEORY OF MULTIPLE INTELLIGENCES

In 1983 Howard Gardner, a professor at Harvard University, published *Frames of Mind: The Theory of Multiple Intelligences*. In this landmark work, Gardner advances the theory that there are numerous ways to conceptualize intelligence. Over the years, he has added to his thinking and now posits that there are even more discreet, identifiable domains than the seven he originally proposed. Gardner believes that our view of intelligence has been too narrow. As a result, people with particular abilities that happen to be highly valued in a given culture are seen as "more intelligent" than those who may have skills and abilities in less-valued areas. Gardner points out that our perception of intelligence may be determined to a large extent by culture. What is valued in one culture, and therefore seen as reflecting intelligence, may not be valued in another culture.

The seven intelligences originally proposed by Gardner are:

- **Logical-mathematical:** This sequential thinker is generally strong in mathematics and problem solving.

- **Spatial:** This thinker has a keen ability to manipulate forms and objects in space.

- **Interpersonal:** This thinker has strong people skills and is good at conflict resolution, listening, and persuasion.

- **Bodily-kinesthetic:** This thinker tends to have good motor skills and values physical and athletic ability.

- **Verbal-linguistic:** This thinker enjoys talking, reading, and most activities that involve using language.

- **Intrapersonal:** This thinker enjoys being alone and is especially skilled at goal setting and self-evaluation.

- **Musical-rhythmic:** This thinker is particularly sensitive to the nuances of sound (timbre, pitch, rhythm).

We each have our own particular pattern of strengths in these domains. The various intelligences are completely independent, so ability in one area doesn't predict ability in another. Gardner's theory of multiple intelligences gives us a new way to conceptualize ability. Jensen (1995, 182) writes, "'How smart are you?' is now irrelevant. A more powerful new question is, 'How are you smart?'"

Our schools have typically put an emphasis on two areas: verbal-linguistic and logical-mathematical. Students skilled in these areas have had the best chance to be successful in school, and school success is a clear advantage in our society. If Gardner's model of multiple intelligences is valid (regardless of the number of intelligences identified), then schools often miss the opportunity to inspire more students. Inspiring teachers work to create learning environments that engage as many intelligences as possible so that greater numbers of students will be inspired to be successful and work hard.

Despite believing in Gardner's theory, I offer this word of caution to teachers. Our society does not yet respect each of the intelligences equally. Part of our job as inspiring teachers is to equip students with the skills that will allow them to participate successfully in our society. For that reason, I suggest a teaching approach that cultivates each of the intelligences but acknowledges and respects the current supremacy of verbal-linguistic and logical-mathematical in our culture.

THE BRAIN-BASED CURRICULUM

When we talk about curriculum, we are talking about content—what is presented to students to learn in a given class or school. Brain-based learning is more concerned with the "how" of teaching than the "what." Virtually any content can be introduced to students in a brain-compatible way. That's essentially what the inspiring teacher does. Concepts are introduced to learners in such a way that they appreciate the value of learning about them and doing their best work. The same content can be introduced in a brain-antagonistic way.

I am less concerned with curricular issues than I am with the other topics that I have discussed in this chapter. Curricular issues are significant, of course, but I spend less time and energy on them for two reasons. First, curricular decisions are often made at a district or even state level. The inspiring teacher who has little or no input into content finds brain-compatible ways to present whatever content is mandated. Second, other books and resources will serve you better in the study of specific curricular issues. I am more concerned with teaching in a brain-based way. For the most part, I leave content to others.

That said, several points about curriculum deserve mention. First, the most compelling curriculum is one that the students perceive as relevant. Since the brain is structured to help us survive, it will attend most to what it perceives as essential. Put simply, if it is not relevant, it is certainly not essential, and students will expend less than optimum energy and effort. Advocates of choice theory and quality schools have long recognized the importance of creating relevant, need-satisfying environments to maximize learning. The relevance needs to be communicated to the learners and appreciated by them. It is not enough that the teacher perceives the curriculum to be meaningful and relevant. It is crucial that the students appreciate the value and relevance of what they are being asked to learn. Inspiring teachers help their students perceive that what they are being asked to learn is valuable to them and worth serious attention and effort. That is the essence of effective managing.

Second, because the brain is a multiprocessor, we learn best when immersed in an interdisciplinary experience. The brain does not process information in a lock-step, sequential way. We take in massive amounts of information and make meaning of it by creating complex webs and connections that blur any lines of subject matter. Natural learning is thematic, interdisciplinary, and efficient. Too much school learning, particularly in secondary schools, is artificially separated into rigid subject categories. If we are serious about improving our schools, we would be wise to look at how we structure our schools and courses of study. It may be convenient to divide the day into periods designated as English, math, social studies, science, art, and music, but this structure doesn't match how the brain is organized. A brain-compatible school offers considerable interdisciplinary work and opportunities for thematic learning.

Third, inspiring teachers generally are more concerned with underlying skills than with specific content. For example, they want students to be able to read well and to become lifelong readers. They are far less concerned about which specific books students read. If they think everyone would profit from reading and discussing particular books, they of course build those books into the curriculum. But, with an understanding of choice theory, they do everything they can to offer students as much choice as possible to satisfy the basic need to be free. When inspiring teachers make the professional decision that certain tasks need to be done, they explain their reasons, helping students appreciate that the tasks makes good sense and are not arbitrary.

Finally, inspiring teachers generally offer students opportunities to learn about various topics in depth. Typically, this strategy translates into less material being covered, but the material that is taught is learned well. In a school organized around the principles of choice theory and brain-based learning, teachers and students take pride in what has been learned, not what has been "covered."

In summary, keep the following in mind when you make curricular decisions:

1. Make the curriculum relevant.

2. Make the curriculum interdisciplinary.

3. Focus on skills.

4. Offer students as much choice as possible.

5. Provide in-depth learning opportunities.

Beyond these general comments, I leave it to each inspiring teacher to determine what is best offered in any given classroom.

EVALUATION

Evaluation is one of the most difficult areas for me to discuss. I believe that we evaluate far too much, using valuable time that would be better spent teaching and learning. Our traditional system of assigning letter grades to students strikes me as one of the least enlightened and most brain-antagonistic notions ever created. As I noted in *Inspiring Quality in Your School* (Sullo 1997, 182), I look forward to a time when we have abolished letter grades and use a system that provides meaningful feedback to students and their parents about what appears to have been learned according to the evidence available to the teacher at a given point in time.

While my comments about typical evaluation and grading may seem radical to some, they are supported by brain research. Eric Jensen (1996, 118) writes, "Many educators think they measure learning every day. They don't. Neuroscientist Gary Lynch of the University of California at Irvine says learning is defined by synaptic growth, connections among dendrites and changes in the density of neural networks. Do you have a test that measures that? Biologist Ira Black...says that learning is defined by 'modifications to the neuronal pattern of connectivity.' Do you have a test that measures that?" Jensen (1995, 277) also notes, "Biologically, the best, most valuable and deepest learning does not produce any tangible results for a considerable time. In other words, most assessment is off course."

One of the most brain-antagonistic practices is comparing one student with another. Fortunately, it's less common today. If there is anything valuable in that process, it certainly has little to do with learning. For those who continue to believe that we need to evaluate students, the only relevant comparative data is how the performance of a particular student compares with what that student produced at some previous time. Students, teachers, and parents can use such information constructively.

I realize that we will probably continue to evaluate student performance, even though I would prefer we limit ourselves to providing feedback designed to help learners effectively self-evaluate and improve the quality of their work. Given the current circumstances, inspiring teachers develop authentic, relevant assessment tools that enhance learning. The most authentic assessments include demonstrations of how students can use what they have learned. Students should be able to articulate in some fashion how the learning has changed them. A tangible product may show others what has been mastered. A well-built bookcase crafted by a student who previously did not have the skills to build one, for example, is tangible evidence that learning has taken place. A letter to a local politician that gets an answer is evidence that a student can express ideas in writing with a measurable degree of competence. A research-based report is evidence that a student knows how to gather, analyze, evaluate, and present information.

Many "real-life" experiences have a built-in feedback system that lets us know whether we have been successful. Much of what we do in schools is less real life, but in no way is it less valuable a pursuit. Inspiring teachers develop clear indicators of quality. When criteria are clearly articulated, and teachers take time to fully instruct students in how to master the required skills, assessment can then be done in a way that provides valuable feedback and enhances the learning of all students.

SUMMARY

Brain-based learning provides inspiring teachers with strategies to create classroom experiences and learning plans that are compatible with how the brain learns most easily and efficiently. Choice theory presents a theoretical model from which to operate. Brain-based learning is an evolving, research-driven model about how we learn. Together with an understanding of the important developmental issues addressed in the next chapter, they provide the foundation on which inspiring teachers can build their classrooms. Using a sound theory of human behavior, linking it with the most current information about how the brain works, and creating a classroom sensitive to the developmental needs of learners gives every teacher a chance to become someone special in the lives of students.

CHAPTER 4

Developmental Issues

Stephen Covey (1989) tells a story about an experience he had while riding the subway in New York. A man and his children entered the quiet subway car where he was sitting. The children began running up and down the car with little parental supervision. Covey believed that the children's father was an ineffective parent. Upset, he spoke to the father and discovered that the family had just left the hospital after learning that the children's mother died. Given this new information, Covey developed a completely different perception of the father and the children's behavior.

We often think that what we infer from our observation is "the" truth. Several truths, however, might explain an observed behavior equally well. Like Covey, teachers may make erroneous judgments when they are working with incomplete information.

Regardless of what age group you teach, you will be faced with a vast array of behaviors every day. Brain researchers have suggested that typical students in a classroom, those not identified with significant developmental challenges or handicaps, can vary developmentally by as much as three years (Jensen 1995, 12). Inspiring teachers possess a solid grasp of developmental issues and an understanding of both the expected and the atypical behaviors expressed at certain ages.

A number of developmental models have been proposed over the years. Robert Kegan (1982) has developed a comprehensive model of psychological development. It suggests that we move through alternating stages of cooperation and competition. We enter each new stage at a higher level than the previous one. As we cycle through the cooperative and competitive stages, our behavior becomes more complex and mature.

Other valuable theories of human development have been presented. Some refer to the cooperative drive as "affiliation." The complementary drive that leads us to separate is sometimes referred to as "individuation." Nancy Buck (1997) has proposed a developmental model that incorporates the ideas of other models and views human development from a choice theory perspective.

A THEORY OF HUMAN DEVELOPMENT

Buck's theory suggests that we are born with genetic instructions, or basic needs, but without the behaviors needed to follow those instructions. We begin our lives dependent on others, specifically our parents or other primary caregivers. We are driven, however, to learn how to provide for ourselves so that we can move from dependence to independence. At least initially, our capacity to develop strong relationships with our caregivers (love and belonging) ensures that we will be provided for during our period of dependence. At the same time, we need to develop the ability to compete so that we will have the behaviors we will need to survive independently in the world. In short, two categories of learning, seemingly contradictory but really complementary, are critical for us in childhood: the ability to cooperate and the ability to compete. Both are necessary behaviors in helping us move toward independence.

Buck explains that the need for love and belonging and

the need for fun are best conceptualized as cooperative needs because we usually use cooperative behaviors to satisfy them. Power and freedom, on the other hand, are competitive needs because we usually use competitive behaviors to satisfy them. While we seek ways to satisfy both our cooperative and competitive needs, throughout childhood there are some periods when we are driven more by cooperation and others when we are driven more by competition.

Buck's model proposes typical age ranges for the developmental stages, but they are only general guidelines. More important is the cyclic movement between the drives to cooperate and compete.

The primary need during the first eight months of life is survival. Assuming that infants feel safe, they are able to attend to the psychological needs to cooperate (love and belonging, fun) and to compete (power, freedom).

From about 8 months to 16 months, infants and toddlers focus more on cooperative behaviors that help them survive and be satisfied. Infants, for example, learn how to coo, smile, make eye contact, and play peekaboo, all effective cooperative behaviors that maximize their chances of being well cared for during this period of dependence.

Between about 16 and 20 months, most toddlers enter the "terrible twos," a period where competitive behaviors become dominant. During this stage, which typically lasts about six months, toddlers express a strong desire for freedom. Lacking the capacity to articulate their needs with words, they scream, have tantrums, and throw objects. Children learn that sometimes they can get what they want by being competitive as well as by being cooperative. So while parents usually do not regard this period with particular fondness, it is an important phase in children's development. Children need to begin acquiring responsible competitive behaviors. People who only learn how to meet their needs using cooperative behaviors are seriously limited as adults.

This cycle continues throughout early childhood. Approximately every six months, children move from a more cooperative phase, dominated by the need for love and belonging and the need for fun, to a more competitive phase, dominated by the need for power and the need for freedom. At each phase, children become more skilled and sophisticated, expanding their repertoires of cooperative and competitive behaviors.

Neither the cooperative nor the competitive approach is wholly satisfying. Cooperating keeps us too close to home and too safe. We're unable to fully explore the world. On the other hand, competing keeps us apart from others. This dynamic drives the cycle throughout childhood. During all phases, children retain the desire to satisfy all their psychological needs, both the more cooperative and the more competitive. One type of need is simply more dominant during a given phase and less dominant during another. Buck suggests, however, that children will often abandon competitive behaviors during a competitive phase if they feel their safety is threatened. They will revert to cooperative behaviors that they believe will be more effective. This strategy has important classroom implications. In fear-laden classrooms, children may behave more cooperatively, but a cost is associated with that behavior. Children give up the exploring, reaching-out, and risk-taking behaviors associated with freedom, power, and increased academic achievement. Inspiring teachers evaluate whether their classroom environments support children when they are in the competitive phase while also providing sufficient structure so that this drive can be followed safely and respectfully.

The six-month cycles continue for roughly the first seven years. Phases then expand and last eight, nine, or ten months, giving children more time to practice the behaviors that will allow them to be more effectively cooperative or competitive.

As children move into adolescence, the competitive behaviors are especially important. They question authority, sometimes in unpleasant ways. Inspiring teachers may not care for some of the behaviors, but they are aware that the primary developmental task of adolescence is separation and the formation of an independent identity. Inspiring teachers perceive the behavior of adolescents for what it is—an attempt to separate, to identify themselves, and to flourish in a developmental phase in which competitive behaviors tend to dominate.

Even during the time when competitive drives are particularly strong, adolescents still feel the cooperative urges. For this reason, many adolescents look very different from their parents (competition) but very much like many of their peers (cooperation). Many adolescents also want the approval of their parents and teachers. Not knowing how to communicate this desire without compromising their independence, they stay more distant from adults than necessary. Inspiring teachers help adolescents feel safe and connected even as they move toward increased separation and independence, sometimes in awkward, challenging ways.

The competitive drive is especially strong in early adolescence. By the time most students reach age 16, cooperative behaviors begin to reemerge, and students use them almost as regularly as competitive behaviors. Teachers who work with students in middle school and the early high school years need to be especially skilled in dealing with students in the competitive phase. Less-skilled teachers either will be discouraged by the difficulty of dealing with students in the midst of a competitive cycle, or they will use "power-over" behaviors, which may shut down students' drive to learn to compete fairly and effectively. In both cases, somebody loses.

If you want to work with students from middle school through the first half of high school, you will need to create a task-oriented, academically focused learning environment that both supports students' drive toward competitive behaviors, autonomy, and separation and maintains your position of authority. One key element is being secure about your own sense of power. Teachers dealing with students who are in the competitive phase are more vulnerable to being drawn into power struggles and arguments. Only teachers who have effective ways of meeting their own need for power are able to manage this situation well. Others get into arguments, even shouting matches with adolescents. They use their authority to get power over students. While this approach provides the teacher with some measure of satisfaction, it models inappropriate behaviors and prevents adolescents from engaging in the crucial developmental task before them: learning how to compete fairly and effectively.

The skills necessary to be an inspiring teacher differ depending on the age of the students and their developmental level. During my 25 years in education, I have worked with prekindergarten to high school students. I have developed a deep respect for what teachers at each level do to inspire their students to produce quality academic work. As Buck's model of human development suggests, teachers working with pre-adolescent students and students nearing the end of high school will face both cooperative phases and competitive phases. Those working with students from early adolescence through about age 16 will find them driven more by competition than by cooperation. Clearly, it is easier to work with others when they are driven by cooperation. Regardless, if you want to be an inspiring teacher, you need to understand what drives students, what needs or tendencies are most pressing at any point in time, and how to structure a developmentally appropriate learning environment.

STAGES OF MORAL REASONING

Lawrence Kohlberg's ideas concerning the development of moral reasoning are among the most important in psychology. Kohlberg proposes that we pass through stages in our moral development. Thomas Lickona (1983) builds on Kohlberg's contributions. Inspiring teachers will find Lickona's work useful for two reasons.

First, it provides a snapshot of typical student behaviors at various ages and stages. Inspiring teachers need to know which behaviors are developmentally expected and which might warrant special attention or intervention.

Second, it provides suggestions about how to move children gently forward to a more advanced stage of moral reasoning. I am in no way advocating that we try to hurry children through the normal developmental process. David Elkind (1981, 1984, 1987) has written eloquently and extensively about the dangers of hurrying children.

Stage One: The Preschool and Kindergarten Years

The preschool and kindergarten stage generally emerges between four and a half and five and a half years old. (Other stages precede this one, but they are outside the scope of this book.) Like Buck, Lickona stresses that age ranges are only approximate guidelines. Despite being approximations, the guidelines are helpful when inspiring teachers are trying to identify typical behavior for a large group of students at a given age and stage.

The typical behavior of children at this stage is characterized by obedience and cooperation. Children's moral reasoning is based on a belief that only one viewpoint, that of adults, is valid. Not surprisingly, children at this age think somewhat primitively. Their compliant behavior follows from a simple premise: we obey so that we will not be punished. They tend to obey because they believe that adults are all-knowing and misbehavior will be discovered. In this stage, children are likely to tattle frequently. They genuinely believe that rules should be followed. They often violate rules, however, when adults are not present and the threat of punishment is removed because they have not internalized the rules. If you ask children at this stage why they should follow rules, they refer to the need to avoid punishment. This perception is generally true even for those children who have experienced little punishment and have been raised in environments that minimize coercion.

The moral reasoning of young children suggests that they are amenable to an approach based on external control psychology. They follow rules because of a fear of punishment, an external orientation. They have yet to internalize rules. Some might argue that this behavior suggests we are externally, not internally, motivated. We should not confuse human motivation with behavior. Children at this stage are internally motivated by their quality world pictures to be obedient, adult pleasing, and compliant. One of the tasks of inspiring teachers is to help children construct more complex quality world pictures. To this end, inspiring teachers help children appreciate the value of the rules we have.

Inspiring teachers do what they can to help children move comfortably to the next stage of moral reasoning. Kohlberg believes that people have the capacity to understand and profit from a moral argument that is one level higher than the one at which they currently operate (Lickona 1983). Anything higher is of no value, since the type of thinking involved is too complex to be understood. The next stage of moral reasoning for preschool to kindergarten children emphasizes the importance of fairness. To help children move forward, we help them begin to develop a capacity to empathize, to imagine what it is like to be on the receiving end of an unkind comment or a wayward fist. For children at this stage, it is important to keep concepts concrete. Appealing to abstractions—for example, saying, "I would like everyone in this class to be treated fairly"—will be of no value to most of them. Instead, ask the children, "How would we all act in this classroom if we treated one another fairly?" This approach moves an abstract concept—fairness—into a concrete domain capable of being understood by young students.

Inspiring teachers avoid comments that appeal to the lowest levels of moral reasoning. The teacher who says, "I never want to catch anyone in this class acting that way!" is appealing to the lowest level of moral reasoning: obey to avoid punishment. Quite unintentionally, the comment suggests that not getting caught is what matters.

Young children do not yet have the capacity to understand "why." For example, they may not be able to understand why stealing is wrong. That's developmentally normal. Still, this inability does not excuse the behavior of stealing or prevent us from using our moral authority to teach them more concretely that stealing is wrong. Of course, to approach something from a position of moral authority requires that the inspiring teacher develop positive relationships with children. We need to behave genuinely, model what we teach, and earn the right to legitimately claim things to be so when children are not yet able to appreciate why such a point of view is reasonable.

Stage Two: The Early Elementary Years

Most children have moved into stage two by the time they are seven or eight years old. Lickona suggests that stage two can last a long time. Although children develop more advanced ways of reasoning, they resort to stage two tendencies with some regularity throughout childhood and adolescence. "Stage Two is alive and well in most of us adults," Lickona (1983, 134) observes.

In stage two, the rule-bound, compliant child from stage one has been replaced by a child driven more by a need for freedom, independence, and individuality. Especially because youngsters lack many socially valued behaviors, this drive toward independence is generally accompanied by a host of challenging behaviors. Inspiring teachers who work with these children are successful in part because they recognize the developmental process that initiates this stage and understand that children are limited by what they know how to do. Any time inspiring teachers work with children in more challenging stages, they are comforted by remembering that all behavior is purposeful and all of us, including young children, are doing the best we can. The inspiring teacher appreciates what children are attempting to do and assists them in developing responsible behaviors to achieve their goals.

While stage one children are generally unable to appreciate more than one point of view, stage two children operate from the position that everyone has an individual point of view. As a result, they believe it is acceptable for people to do what they want to do and to ask, "What's in it for me?" Children at this stage are demanding and egocentric. They see themselves as equal to adults in many ways and begin to assert that they have rights. They are likely to resist anything they see as "bossing" them.

Fairness is a major concern for students in this stage. Because they are young and think concretely, stage two thinkers define fairness as everyone getting the same treatment. They are consummate dealmakers. "I'll be nice to you if you are nice to me" makes perfect sense to them. Being nice is not valued in itself. It is valued because relationships should be reciprocal. Of course, the reverse works equally well for stage two thinkers: "If you are not nice to me, it is only fair that I am not nice to you."

Fairness is an especially important issue for teachers with classrooms that are increasingly heterogeneous. Inspiring teachers discover ways to provide for the diverse needs of students with vastly different levels of ability while respecting the stage two demand for equality. The task is difficult, but inspiring teachers have been successfully undertaking it for years. I can't tell you the "right" way for you to meet this challenge, but I will offer some thoughts about how to proceed.

It is crucial for inspiring teachers to appreciate that stage two thinkers perceive fairness as equality and that they highly value this concept. In an effort to engage the students and respect their developmental level, address the issue of fairness openly. You can create a shared quality world vision by explaining that fairness is important to you. A simple declaration will do much to help you build positive relationships with your students. Next, you might help stage two thinkers develop an expanded notion of what fairness means. Rick Lavoie (How Difficult Can This Be? 1989), director of the Riverview School in Sandwich, Massachusetts, explains in his presentations, "Fairness does not mean that everyone gets the same thing. Fairness means that everyone gets what he or she needs."

All of us move back and forth between various stages throughout our lives. As Lickona notes, many adults sometimes operate from a stage two perspective. Some teachers have a stage two perception that fairness only means equal treatment. This perception makes it difficult to teach heterogeneous classes and serve special-needs students in regular education classes. These teachers could be more successful by expanding their definition of fairness to mean that we all get what we need.

Because stage two students are both more assertive and less fearful of adults, they have the capacity to engage in blatantly mean behavior. Such behavior is developmentally expected and fairly predictable. The preoccupation with fairness, defined in narrow terms, leads students to get into more confrontations, since they frequently are incapable of letting go of their negative emotions without first dispensing suitable payback. Of course, we don't allow students to be nasty to each other. Understanding that we can only control our own behavior, we ask these questions when we encounter inappropriate and sometimes outrageous behavior by students: "What can I do to help these students successfully negotiate this developmental phase? What is the most helpful way for me to perceive them and their behavior? What can I say to these students and do with them that will help them move forward in a socially appropriate and respectful way?" We focus less on imposing "consequences"—although there may be consequences—than on assisting students through a natural developmental process.

Another way to manage nasty behavior is to appeal to students' sense of fairness. Because fairness is central in the quality worlds of stage two thinkers, an appeal to fairness will at least be entertained. When appealing to fairness takes you only so far and stage two thinkers are stuck in an unhelpful way of conceptualizing fairness, you can gently invite them to move forward by stressing that love is an even more important value than fairness. Students will only be moved by this concept if two conditions are present. First, you need to have solid relationships with them. You are, after all, asking them to go beyond their most developmentally compelling value. Without the benefit of positive relationships, there is little reason to believe that you can move students beyond their current view. Second, you need to model that you value love more than fairness. Teachers traditionally, and appropriately, value fairness. If you are asking your students to demonstrate allegiance to another value, they will be quick to evaluate whether you have behaved in a way that suggests love is a higher value than fairness. What they have seen from you will go a long way in determining how seriously they consider your invitation to move forward.

Stage Three: The Middle Elementary Years and Beyond

Stage three is in many ways the most interesting stage of moral reasoning because of its complexity. Some students begin to move into this stage during the middle elementary years, but others don't begin until much later. Stage three is characterized by trying to please others. Depending on when this stage emerges, a stage three approach to moral reasoning can be a welcome change or just another nightmare.

If students begin to move into a stage three orientation before adolescence, adults are usually ecstatic. There is a return of obedience, a desire to please and to conform to expectations. In school, these students are more easily managed. If, however, students move into stage three at the onset of adolescence, its manifestations are quite different. The desire to please is just as strong, but the reference point becomes the peer group, not parents and teachers. As a result, stage three adolescents may lack the strength to stand up for themselves. They may fall prey to peer pressure in unhelpful, perhaps dangerous, ways.

Stage three thinkers are concerned about how others see them. They work diligently to gain approval. While that statement may sound like an endorsement of external control psychology, the desire to be thought of positively by others is in the quality worlds of stage three thinkers, so they are very much internally motivated.

One of the most appealing qualities of stage three thinkers is their ability to see things from another's viewpoint. In part because they are so focused on what others think of them, they are particularly skilled in appreciating how others feel. As a result, they are often particularly generous and compassionate. They have moved beyond a narrow understanding of fairness and have developed the capacity to be more flexible and creative. Stage three thinkers are comfortable when the teacher has different sets of expectations for students and gives them individualized evaluations.

Inspiring teachers respectfully capitalize on stage three thinkers' desire to cooperate. Appealing to students' internal motivation, they ask questions such as the following: "Would you like to be known as someone who is honest, hard working, and responsible?" Further, instead of resorting to using power and imposing consequences, inspiring teachers vigorously work with these students to resolve problems collaboratively. Stage three thinkers especially appreciate this approach. They want to cooperate, and problem solving is a developmentally appropriate task for adolescents.

During adolescence, students naturally want more independence. Inspiring teachers don't struggle against what is developmentally written into our genes. On the other hand, they realize that a certain amount of adult authority is needed for classrooms to be academically productive. Inspiring teachers allow considerable freedom within a well-structured environment that the students have endorsed as reasonable and worth supporting.

Stage Four: Adolescents and Adults

Stage four represents a significant shift in thinking from the strictly personal relationships of stage three to an emphasis on relationship to an entire system. Stage three thinkers seek approval, so they are likely to succumb to peer pressure to maintain personal relationships. At stage four, students are concerned about being good members of this class, this school, this gang, this clique, this larger society. The capacity to move beyond individual relationships and into the realm of social relationships means that these students are able to enter into a social contract. Stage three thinkers are more likely to be conformers, behaving in ways to gain peer approval. Stage four thinkers are more invested in behaving responsibly toward the system in which they operate. Stage four thinking is at the heart of our democratic government. It is what allows us to put aside our personal desires for the good of the larger society. In this stage, students develop the capacity to move beyond simple independence toward interdependence.

Another major shift for students at this stage is their capacity to appreciate that their actions affect many others. At earlier stages of moral reasoning, students behave with less sensitivity in part because they are unable to understand just how much their individual actions are part of a larger whole and have widespread ramifications. Stage four students can generate heartfelt emotion and passion for people with whom they have no personal relationship, provided those people are part of the same system.

Stage four thinkers value the need to cooperate, although they have the ability to behave in uncooperative ways. Inspiring teachers can appeal to stage four thinkers' belief in the importance of cooperation for the good of the system. Those students who achieve stage four understand what is involved in being a functioning member of a larger system. Finally, stage four thinkers want a system of belief upon which they can base their decisions.

Some of the best and most successful social institutions and businesses thrive because of stage four thinking. The United States itself is built upon stage four moral reasoning. The Constitution serves as the belief system against which we measure and evaluate our actions. While we are a nation of individuals, we believe as a nation that no person is above the law and the principles set forth in our Constitution. Many schools and businesses are moving toward a similar way of operating. Mission statements and belief statements become the documents by which actions are considered, evaluated, and taken.

The further we move along the continuum of moral reasoning, the more differentiation we encounter and the more difficult it is to approximate when students will begin to display the behaviors typical of a given stage. Many students, as well as adults, never move beyond a stage three orientation. Still, given the right environment, many teenagers can begin moving toward a stage four orientation. Some even begin to demonstrate signs of this type of moral reasoning during the middle school years. Inspiring teachers have no capacity to control the homes in which students live. They do, however, have the ability to create school and classroom environments that support and enhance the moral reasoning skills of students.

Inspiring teachers guide their students toward stage four moral reasoning in many ways. They can help students realize that the world is vast and that we are increasingly interdependent. As students acquire information about the world at large, they will gradually become more sensitive, knowledgeable, and appreciative of those around them. Inspiring teachers can also facilitate regular discussions about social and moral issues, allowing students to think about the relationship between the individual and any larger system (class, school, team, community). Such discussions naturally lead to considering what it means to be a responsible person. Inspiring teachers avoid moralizing or telling students what they "should" do, preferring that students develop responsibility by coming to their own conclusions.

Stage five, the highest level of moral reasoning, is based on respect for the rights of each individual and the belief that none of us can ever abdicate our moral responsibility. Because so few people ever reach this stage or operate from this perspective regularly, and because individuals rarely attain this stage until they are in their twenties or beyond, I will not address it here. Lickona (1983) provides thorough information about stage five, as well as a treatment of how to apply the concepts in parenting.

The development of moral reasoning, a critically important area, is often overlooked in education. Inspiring teachers strive to prepare students to become positive contributors to our society and our world. Teaching academics is essential, but it is not sufficient. Our mission as educators is to prepare students who have the skills, both academic and social, to take their place as citizens in a democratic society. Understanding the stages of moral reasoning and developing strategies that enhance a student's development are indispensable tools for inspiring teachers.

STAGES OF COGNITIVE DEVELOPMENT

Much of what we know about cognitive development we owe to Swiss psychologist Jean Piaget. Although many others have made significant contributions and built upon the foundation he provided, Piaget remains one of the most important names in the field of cognition.

Piaget's greatest contribution to our understanding of children and their cognitive development can be expressed simply: children think *differently* from adults. Until Piaget's ideas gained considerable attention in the 1950s, children were generally thought to have less knowledge than adults but to process information in the same way.

Piaget's contributions are congruent with the teachings

of choice theory and the belief that we actively construct meaning from our experiences using our current knowledge. Because young children have a different set of experiences from adults, they process information differently and construct very different meaning from identical input.

The fact that children process and create so differently from adults underscores the limitations of spoken language. While we appear to speak the same language as children, we often are communicating and understanding in different ways. Communication through spoken language is always a high-risk endeavor. Communication through spoken language between child and adult has tremendous potential for misinterpretation. Inspiring teachers seek to communicate clearly with students. When errors in communication occur, they accept that they are as much to blame as the child is.

Piaget is most widely known for having developed a four-stage model of cognitive development (Biehler 1981). Like other theorists, he stresses that the age ranges for his stages are merely guidelines. The sequence of cognitive development, however, is predictable. Children drift between stages, moving ahead or regressing from time to time.

Piaget's first stage, the *sensorimotor stage,* occurs during the first two years of life. The first stage of direct concern to teachers is called the *preoperational stage.* It is typical of children from about two to seven years old. The primary cognitive task during the preoperational stage is the mastery of symbols. That is why language develops so rapidly during this particular period. An important quality of children at this stage is the tendency to center their attention on only one variable when solving problems. For example, children who are shown that two containers of different heights hold equal amounts of water will still insist that the taller container holds more.

Sometime around the age of seven, students move into the *concrete operational stage* of cognitive development. For most, it lasts until early adolescence. To learn effectively, students at this stage need to physically manipulate objects or to have had direct, concrete experience with them. Under these conditions, students are able to mentally reverse actions, something they were unable to do at the preoperational stage. Concrete operational thinkers will be confounded by hypothetical situations and will struggle with abstractions. For example, they may do well when learning geometry, a highly visual subject area, especially if they have been given opportunities to create tangible models. These same students, highly motivated and academically capable, might then struggle with algebra unless the teacher can transform this abstract subject into something concrete.

Beginning about age 12, many students show behaviors characteristic of *formal operational* thinking, the most complex thinking Piaget postulated. During middle school and even high school, students move back and forth between concrete operational and formal operational thinking. Their erratic performance and behavior can be frustrating for some adults, but inspiring teachers understand that such is the nature of typical human development.

Formal operational thought is characterized by an ability to generalize, to engage in abstract thinking, and to develop and test hypotheses mentally. Inspiring teachers help students develop the capacity to deal successfully with abstractions while respecting that some students still require a more concrete orientation.

Inspiring teachers create environments that offer challenges and opportunities for students who may be operating at different cognitive stages. Piaget's contribution to the field of education relates to how children at different stages take in and make sense of information. Nothing in Piaget's model suggests a particular curriculum or limits what is taught. Inspiring teachers using Piaget's work understand that *how* instruction is delivered is as important as the intellectual potential of the students. Intelligent students who are provided instruction that is not matched to their cognitive stage will not progress as well as those who may be less gifted but who have been given appropriate instruction.

STAGES OF PSYCHOSOCIAL DEVELOPMENT

Erik Erikson provides an eight-stage model of psychosocial development (Biehler 1981). Many of the stages involve the preschool years or the years after high school. I will discuss only two of Erikson's stages here.

Children between the ages of approximately 6 to 11 fall into the stage Erikson terms *industry vs. inferiority.* The developmental task during the elementary years is to develop a sense of industry. Students who are unable to do so are likely to develop feelings of inferiority and become chronic underachievers.

During the industry vs. inferiority stage, the need for power or competence is a primary concern. Schools are especially important during this phase because the classroom is one arena where the need for power can be satisfied in a responsible, growth-enhancing way. Inspiring teachers create classrooms that encourage students to demonstrate competence, master skills, and build a sense of industry that will serve them well for the rest of their lives. Students who don't experience academic success in their elementary school years rarely experience it in secondary school. Students who develop a capacity to work hard and achieve during elementary school are better equipped to meet the challenges offered in secondary school.

From about 12 to 18 years old, students are in the stage termed *identity vs. role confusion.* The central task of adolescence is the formation of a stable identity. The identity we each establish is what makes us unique and recognizable despite all the physical changes that may occur over time. If we are unable to establish a stable sense of identity, we go through life like a rudderless ship, lacking a sense of who we are and continually reinventing ourselves.

One of the first signs that students are entering this phase is the establishment of crude preliminary identities. Previously, students identified with their parents and embraced many adult values. Now, they want to distinguish themselves from adults in general and their parents in particular. Students often adopt identities that are the opposite of their parents'. Essentially, students devalue everything their parents value. What is frequently perceived as adolescent rebelliousness can be seen as an attempt to differentiate, to begin the process of separation that culminates in the formation of a genuine identity. Because early adolescents have limited behavioral repertoires, they often focus on the opposite: "I may not be sure exactly what I want to be or who I want to be, but I know that I don't want to be like my parents. Therefore, anything that represents my parents—from clothes to music to political and religious ideas—I will reject, and I will embrace the opposite."

In adopting an extreme stance, many early adolescents achieve the separation they desire. In situations where children have been particularly close to their parents and have blindly accepted parental values, this process can be especially difficult and result in the adoption of what is frequently called a "negative identity," a temporary identity that is completely opposite from the previous one.

Inspiring teachers realize that this temporary identity is normal for many students during the early phases of identity formation. Creating an identity, even a negative one, is preferable to having none at all. Erikson calls for adults not to judge adolescents too quickly or too harshly as they go through this important developmental phase. To use Erikson's language, if we "confirm" the temporary identity by labeling a student a "delinquent," we increase the chances of the student permanently maintaining that identity. It is crucial to separate the student from the behavior.

Suppose an adolescent is caught using an illegal drug. I am not suggesting that we ignore that unsettling reality or that there might not be some unpleasant consequences. Still, inspiring teachers do not label the student a "drug user." Some will find that strategy disturbing. "If a student uses a drug, isn't he a drug user?" they will ask. Of course, but there is no value in using that label. There is tremendous potential for danger when we label adolescent behavior. In essence, it provides the adolescent a way to avoid the primary developmental task of adolescence. Instead of doing the difficult work of forming a true identity, the student is simply able to assume the prepackaged "druggie" identity with little effort. Since having an identity, any identity, is so powerfully attractive to the adolescent, he only needs to continue behaving in the same way and his developmental struggle is over. He no longer has to confront the difficult questions—Who am I? What is important to me? What are my true values?—that hound so many adolescents. Identified as a druggie, the struggle to "become" dissipates.

Adolescents are capable of outrageous behaviors, some of them potentially deadly. These behaviors need to be addressed. Still, never confirm a negative identity. Recognize that adolescents are in the process of becoming. What they ultimately become, the true identities they forge for themselves, will be influenced by how we treat them as they move through this developmental stage. As they try on a host of roles and accompanying behaviors, it is crucial that we remember that they are works in progress. We want students to evolve into adults who are caring, responsible decision-makers. Pierce Howard (1994, 141) suggests, "Be reasonably accepting of selfishness and impulsivity among youth, knowing that—with understanding parents and societal nudging—the tendency is for people in their twenties to move toward a more cooperative and goal-focused adulthood."

It is unlikely that students will have formed their true identities by the time they leave high school. For most of us, the process continues into our twenties even under the best of circumstances. Still, with appropriate adult support, many adolescents can begin building a strong foundation for a unique identity.

GENDER AND GENDER BIAS

Most developmental models, including all but one of the models discussed in this chapter, have been offered by men. Positive intentions notwithstanding, we all bring biases to our work, and male theorists present a male perspective. Carol Gilligan (1993) suggests that the most widely studied developmental models have been proposed by men and do not accurately reflect the developmental process as it relates to women. I therefore encourage you to take the comments offered in this chapter only as general guidelines. Determine what you find useful and add your own knowledge to the mix to enhance what has been written on these pages.

SUMMARY

Helping students successfully move through various developmental stages is one of the most important things we do as educators. Development can be viewed from various perspectives: psychological, moral reasoning, cognitive, and psychosocial. Without an understanding of developmental issues, we can misinterpret the behavior of students and work with them in ways that are both counterproductive and fraught with unnecessary stress and tension. While each child is unique and no one fits any model perfectly, a familiarity with this information will help inspiring teachers do their jobs more effectively.

PART II

Application

CHAPTER 5

Inspiring Your Students

What steps can teachers take to inspire students and create a community of learners? Even the best classroom situations will present challenges. Nevertheless, when the principles of choice theory and brain-based learning are the foundation for building a community of learners, education is an exciting, need-satisfying process for everyone.

BUILDING THE CLASSROOM COMMUNITY

The most important variable in any human interaction is the relationship itself. Education is nothing if not a process based on human relationships. Only people have the ability to inspire learners in great numbers. Computers and other technology might be a wonderful enhancement in the classroom, but no lesson driven by technology can inspire the way a gifted teacher can. A learner who is already interested in a particular subject can be successful when the teaching strategy relies primarily on technology. Given anything less than an interested student, technology cannot teach even reasonably well, much less inspire.

Think about situations in which someone asked you to become involved in a learning task that required hard work. In cases where the work itself was important to you, the relationship between you and the person asking you to do the work was probably not critical. Even if you did not particularly care for the other person, you put forth a strong effort because you valued the work. In choice theory terminology, the work was part of your quality world.

What if you had a positive relationship with the person asking you to work hard? The quality of your work was probably even higher. Your full energy was available for the task at hand instead of being split between the task and thoughts about an unsatisfactory relationship. Furthermore, you probably felt comfortable seeking the other person's assistance if you needed it. While you might not have valued the task initially, a positive relationship with a caring teacher can help you appreciate that what you're being asked to learn will add quality to your life.

Learning is a process of discovery. In a positive environment, we naturally want to learn more, share more, make new connections, and continue the exciting process of discovery. Put simply, a positive relationship does not interfere with the learning process or negatively affect effort. It can only enhance the learning.

In contrast, a negative environment can have dire consequences if learning is the goal, specifically developing a life-long love of learning. Brain-based learning researchers have identified the consequences of threat in the environment (Jensen 1995, 232). When students feel threatened, their motivation, productivity, and achievement decline dramatically. The threat need not be physical. The psychological threat that accompanies sarcasm, criticism, and ridicule is equally damaging.

Inspiring teachers understand the crucial importance of relationships and intentionally foster positive relationships with students from the outset. In some cases, that means building relationships even before the teacher and students are officially connected. For example, many of the teachers in my children's school have taken time to learn the names of all the students. The teachers greet them regardless of the classroom they are in. The dividends that effort pays are enormous. Children, like the rest of us, have a need to be recognized, to feel as if they matter. When a seventh or eighth grade teacher takes the time to find out younger students' names and actually say hello, the students feel important. When those students eventually get to the seventh or eighth grade, how do you think they behave? Not surprisingly, they are much less likely to be disruptive, because students generally do not disrupt with adults who have treated them well. Just as important, students are more likely to work harder because a positive relationship has already been established. Many teachers have unintentionally built positive relationships with students before they had them in class and reaped the benefits. The inspiring teacher intentionally takes the first step in building a community of learners.

The most effective behaviors are always genuine. They occur within the context of what ordinarily happens in schools. Sometimes, however, it is impossible to build positive relationships with students ahead of time. For example, a kindergarten teacher likely will have difficulty forming a meaningful connection with children who have not yet entered the building. The same holds true for teachers in other transition grades.

Some teachers and schools have devised ways to help build relationships with students before they officially enter the building. One typical approach is to have students visit their new building during a designated orientation or "step-up" day. Done well, the experience can be a valuable first step in forging positive relationships with incoming students. Done poorly, it can be unproductive and even damaging. Students can leave the experience feeling overwhelmed, scared, and intimidated by the notion of moving to the next level. Inspiring teachers recognize this possibility and make sure they avoid negative experiences.

At the risk of overgeneralizing, I will suggest that negative experiences occur more often at orientation sessions for secondary schools. Often, the orientation becomes a forum for well-meaning, but overbearing, adults to tell incoming students the school's rules and the consequences of violating them. While this information may be important to communicate, I question the wisdom of the timing and tone. Rather, educators should be mindful of the opportunity to begin creating positive relationships with incoming students and do nothing that might compromise that effort. Educators are better served by saying they are looking forward to working and learning together with students, not by intimidating students with threats of what will happen if they don't follow the school's rules.

Another strategy many teachers use to create positive relationships with incoming students is writing each student a letter before the school year begins. Again, this effort can be wonderful or counterproductive. Inspiring teachers remember their objective, their quality world picture: to foster relationships with students that will be free of fear and will lead to the highest academic standards. Driven by that goal, they write friendly and enthusiastic letters. They give students a preview of the wonderful academic opportunities that will greet them when the term starts. The letters contain little or no mention of rules and consequences. The focus is on helping the students see themselves as valued members of a learning community. The letters let students know that they will be challenged and have opportunities to grow, that they will gain new knowledge and develop new skills, and that they will experience the pleasure of working hard and achieving their goals.

A word of caution to any teacher considering writing a letter to students: even if you write a form letter, find a way to personalize it. There is nothing wrong with writing a general letter to the group, but if it lacks a personal touch, its value is compromised. Remember, you are trying to recognize students. How recognized do you feel when you receive a sterile form letter with a computer-generated label? Students are no different. If nothing else, at least address the envelopes by hand. That alone suggests that each student is important enough to get some individual attention. You might also ask the students to think about some things they have done during the vacation that they can share when the group forms. Although everyone gets the same letter, each student reflects on unique experiences.

THE FIRST DAY OF SCHOOL

The more defined your quality world picture is, the easier it is for you to select behaviors that have the greatest likelihood of leading you where you want to go. With that in mind, inspiring teachers have a clear sense of what they want from their students and themselves on the first day of school. The specifics will vary from teacher to teacher. Here are some thoughts about what I want to achieve on the first day.

Since I want to begin creating an environment where students consistently produce quality academic work, I first must make the classroom nonthreatening. Guided by the principles of choice theory and brain-based learning, I know how important it is that students perceive the classroom environment as a place where they are all free to take risks, make mistakes, and grow. In a fear-laden environment, I may get compliance. I may have few disruptions. I may be able to get students to perform reasonably well on assessments that require little serious thinking. But I will never get their best work.

What do I say to my students? I tell them that I have no interest in punishing them. My sole objective is to teach them. Because I value learning and what we will do in our class, I expect they will work hard, but I know at times they will struggle academically. I welcome academic struggles because they are a signal that students are actively engaged in trying to master concepts. I tell my students that confusion, struggle, and frustration indicate that they are moving forward.

As an inspiring teacher, one of my primary jobs is putting learners in the best position to make gains. I want them to view their academic struggles positively. I try to help them move from thinking "I'm frustrated; I just don't understand this" toward "I'm frustrated; that must mean I'm making progress; this is pretty exciting." The second interpretation is as valid as the first and is more constructive educationally.

Some students will also have behavioral struggles, even in the best classrooms. Careful development of classroom rules helps make managing disruptions considerably easier.

I don't believe I've ever met a teacher who doesn't have classroom rules. Most educators suggest that it is wise to involve students in formulating rules. I certainly agree. As I say in my workshops, if there is to be a revolution in the United States, it probably won't begin in Congress. Those who make the rules are the least likely to lead the revolt. Students in your classroom may disrupt on occasion, but there will not be a revolution if they are genuinely involved in creating the rules.

When I was a classroom teacher, I worked reasonably well in creating rules with my students. That's one of the reasons why I had few serious disruptions. In retrospect, though, I see a serious flaw in how I conducted the rule-making discussion on the first day of school. Once we had come to agreement about reasonable rules, I would say, "These are the rules we have all agreed to follow while we are together. Can everybody live with them?" I had no idea how negative my comment must have sounded. I was sending an unintentional message: "Look, I know rules are a nuisance and none of us likes them, but will you tolerate them?" Rules, I implied, were a necessary evil.

Today, I would do things differently. I would still involve the students in developing the rules. I would continue to make sure that the things I value were included on the list of ideas as well. Remember, just because you invite the students to help create the rules, you are still part of the group. You have just as much right as anyone else to have input when ideas are being developed.

Once we finished our list, I would ask the class to combine the ideas so that we had as few rules as possible. The fewer rules there are, the easier it is for everyone to remember them, including you. The classroom will feel less like a prison and more like the exciting learning environment you are trying to foster.

Some may think that asking the students to distill their ideas into a few general rules is a waste of valuable academic time. On the contrary, it is an important academic pursuit involving the skills of editing, summarizing, discriminating, and negotiating. The process will enable you to teach more and your students to learn more as the school year unfolds.

I now know that it's important for students to value classroom rules and put them into their quality worlds. I would no longer say, "Can you live with these?" I would want my students to say, "These rules are good for us, and we're glad we have them." If we appreciate rules, we are much more likely to internalize them, to follow them even when we are not being watched. We are also likely to accept any consequences of violating the rules without a lot of fussing.

CREATING A SUPPORTIVE ENVIRONMENT

Inspiring teachers are primarily concerned with developing an environment conducive to learning as the school year begins. While serious academic work begins immediately in a quality classroom, the emphasis is on intentionally creating a positive learning environment because it will lead to greater academic achievement as the school year unfolds.

Jon Erwin is a friend and colleague who now works as a staff development specialist in New York. When Jon was an English teacher, he gave his high school students a test on the opening day of school. It was a diagnostic test, but it was far different from a typical diagnostic test. It helped his students experience just how much Jon believed in the value of creating genuine involvement with his students.

The test was 20 multiple-choice questions about Jon. How long had Jon been a teacher? What kind of music did he enjoy? What were his favorite books and movies? How many siblings did he have? The purpose of the experience was both to humanize Jon for his students and to help them realize that they knew little about him. He was more than "the English teacher," whatever that term meant to each of them.

As a follow-up experience, Jon had students create tests about themselves. When students "corrected" the tests, they learned some interesting things about each other-- some overtly academic, others less directly related to school. All helped build a supportive classroom environment.

THIS CLASS WAS GREAT!

One of the first tasks for inspiring teachers and their students is to create a shared vision of a quality classroom experience. On the first day of school, ask the students to imagine that the school year (or the course) is over. The class went even better than they might have hoped. They learned a tremendous amount of useful information. Ask them to describe what they learned and what they did that led them to say, "This class was great!" (Some inspiring teachers might decide to have the students put their thoughts in writing, another way to make an important academic task meaningful to students.) Inspiring teachers participate in this visioning activity, demonstrating that they are a part of the group, albeit in a specific leadership role. They clearly articulate to the students both what a great class sounds like and looks like and what students would never hear and never see.

DEVELOPING ROLES IN A QUALITY CLASSROOM

After completing the visioning activity, students are ready to make the vision come to life. One key step is defining roles within the classroom. Diane Gossen, a nationally known staff developer, has created an activity that helps students appreciate the importance of defining roles and behaving in ways consistent with those roles.

Explain to the class that it's important for everyone to fully understand the student's job and the teacher's job. The students will be working together as a group for an extended time, and they have developed a vision of what they want from this classroom experience. When students know exactly what they are expected to do, they have a better chance of being successful. If they don't know what they're supposed to do, it's almost impossible for a teacher to inspire quality.

In discussing these ideas, you should use language that's comfortable for you. You might say the following to your students: "In order for us to be able to say, 'This class was great!' we need to figure out what each of us should do. We all have responsibilities in this classroom, and I think it will be helpful if we can determine exactly what your job is and what my job is. It's also important to me that we identify what is not my job and what is not your job. We are doing this so that we can work together in the best possible way and leave here saying, 'This class was great!'"

Now it's time to brainstorm with your students. Create a chart that looks like this:

Teacher's Job	Student's Job
is _____	is _____
is not _____	is not _____

As the class completes the chart, you and your students will be involved in the dynamic process of defining roles. During the school year, you can always refer back to the teacher's job/student's job and visioning activities when you give assignments and behave in all the ways managers do. Your students will more likely see the importance and relevance of your requests. Fewer students will ask, "Why do we have to do this?" and more will put forth the serious effort required to do quality work.

WORKING WITH A PURPOSE

It is wise for teachers to engage in activities that are directly related to the subject matter being studied as soon as the school year begins. Inspiring teachers do not spend too much time on activities that are unrelated to academics. What separates inspiring teachers from those who are less skilled is that inspiring teachers are initially less concerned about academic results and more concerned about how well the group is forming and how successfully a positive learning environment is being created. Other teachers may give their students the same work, but their focus is on how well the students do in a narrowly defined academic way. Inspiring teachers notice students' achievement, but they are initially more interested in how the students work. Do they work diligently? Are students committed to quality, or is their work simply completed with little regard to the quality? If some students are struggling, do others offer appropriate assistance, or is the classroom characterized by a "survival of the fittest" mentality? Are students working toward forming a whole group, or are there cliques and isolates within the group? Inspiring teachers know that these and related environmental issues will play a significant role in how much genuine learning occurs during the year.

Once a positive learning environment has been built, it takes relatively little effort to maintain. The teacher's energy can then be directed more overtly toward student learning and achievement. As the school year unfolds, inspiring teachers are vigilant about the academic progress and struggles of students. Notably, learning in the classroom is enhanced by internal motivation, peer support, and a classroom culture in which effort and achievement are the rule, not the exception.

EVERYBODY IS IMPORTANT: GENUINE INCLUSION

Part of building the environment involves creating a belief that you value each student and everybody has something positive to contribute to learning. Too many classes are stratified already. Some students are identified as "winners," those who are bright or play the school game well, or both. Others are the "losers," the disenfranchised students who rarely do quality work and frequently disrupt the learning of others. In the middle is a large amorphous group that could go either way. As classes become more diverse and students previously educated in separate settings are placed in regular education classes, discovering ways to manage potentially destructive stratification becomes increasingly important.

Inspiring teachers are capable of creating classrooms where all students believe they are valued and have something positive to contribute to the group. They start by personally believing that all students are valuable and do have something positive to contribute, regardless of who the students are or what educational handicap they might have. Inspiring teachers are not naive. They do not believe that all students learn in the same way or that all students will learn the same amount. They do believe that all students can learn. When students put forth serious effort and make academic gains, they feel good about themselves as learners and appreciate the opportunity to contribute positively to the class. Students who are genuinely valued, not patronized, and are given a challenging, but manageable environment will be inspired to do their best work. Not all will learn the same amount, but all will become involved in a quality educational process and will progress further than they otherwise would have. Inspiring teachers are not magicians or miracle workers. They do, however, help students come closer to achieving their potential.

How do you create a classroom where all learners feel valued? Certainly it is important to tell your students that you value each of them. Don't think, however, that your words alone will convince them. Older students in particular have heard such words for years. Students also need actions demonstrating that you practice what you preach.

Mismatchers: Often Misunderstood

Brain researchers have identified a group of students who learn most easily by searching for differences, exceptions, and discrepancies (Jensen 1995, 259). This group is called mismatchers because its members create meaning by identifying what doesn't fit. While matchers look for similarities, mismatchers look for what violates the regular scheme.

Generally, matchers are more easily managed in traditional classroom settings. They tend to agree and to seek areas of agreement. Mismatchers are more likely to argue and point out discrepancies. Like matchers, they are simply sorting through information in ways that are meaningful to them. Teachers who don't understand this method of learning can easily see mismatchers as disruptive and difficult. Ironically, mismatchers who argue with you are not trying to be disruptive or disrespectful. Their arguing is a sign of their active engagement with the material.

Several years ago, I conducted a week-long workshop for a school's staff. The principal told me that the group was generally positive but that one staff member was especially difficult and would probably challenge everything I suggested. He was right. Fortunately, I conducted this workshop right after I first read about mismatchers. At one time, I would have seen this teacher as a negative force in the group. With new information and a more helpful perception, I realized that this teacher was actively and energetically working to make sense of what I was offering in the workshop. Because I was not threatened by his mismatching, he became an asset to the group. I was able to help the rest of the group understand how his way of processing contributed positively to all of our learning. The mismatcher felt accepted and valued. Consequently, he only spoke when he had something useful to add. He was not driven to speak up constantly in an effort to be heard. The rest of the staff left the workshop with a new appreciation of their colleague. They were better able to take advantage of his considerable wisdom, which they had largely ignored before. As the facilitator, I was pleased that I had modeled a way to include a mismatcher.

The Timid: Include but Don't Overwhelm

Inspiring teachers accept that some students are more extroverted than others. Certain students in any group will naturally be more quiet and timid. In the inclusive classroom, every student is invited to participate, but active participation does not necessarily mean significant verbal contributions. In a classroom where students are fearful of saying anything, something is wrong. On the other hand, it's perfectly acceptable when some students are comfortable participating actively but are simply quieter than others. These students learn more effectively by watching and internally processing as they make meaning. Inspiring teachers appreciate the different learning styles and do not coerce students into ungenuine verbal classroom participation. While inviting all students to participate verbally, they also take steps to ensure that all are able to contribute in their own ways to enhance their learning. Quieter students are not penalized because of their learning style.

Sometimes, of course, verbal participation is a necessary part of the class. Inspiring teachers make sure that all students understand and value its importance. When students perceive the importance of something, they are much more likely to cooperate. Some students will certainly find verbal presentations in front of the class more challenging. Inspiring teachers strive to create an environment where learners are willing to risk stepping out of their comfort zones. In the right setting, most students will try something new.

Learning Teams

Learning teams are another way to help students feel included. By regularly changing group composition, cliques become less of a force, and the class begins to develop more cohesion. Simply putting students in groups is usually not effective. Poorly structured group activities can be destructive. Students need to be taught specific skills for working in a group. The tasks required in any group activity need to be carefully delineated, and students must have the skills to perform the tasks well.

Naive teachers may believe that students walk into the classroom with these group skills in place. They find out quickly that the students often do not know how to work effectively and responsibly. Frequently, powerful students in the groups bully other students. A few students may do most, if not all, of the work while their partners freeload. Less quality learning takes place, and the teacher may decide that learning teams and cooperative activities are a waste of time.

Inspiring teachers are less naive. Even before teaching group skills, they discuss the value of group learning. Then they teach the students how to behave as a team and identify the specific roles involved in the task. (For group learning strategies, see Johnson, Johnson, and Holubec 1993.)

Well-run learning teams capitalize on the various talents that students bring to the classroom. Complex learning tasks are often best done when approached with several kinds of intelligence. Learning teams succeed when they are diverse. Inspiring teachers expect so much from their students that each group needs the talents of all its members. In that situation, every group member feels valued and has a chance to experience the satisfaction that comes from putting forth effort and creating something of quality.

Emphasize Learning More Than Achievement

Another way to create a truly inclusive environment where all feel valued is to emphasize learning rather than achievement. It's naive to expect that all students will achieve at a relatively equal rate. Brain researchers know that the abilities of typical students can vary by as much as three years within any one grade (Jensen 1995, 12). That three-year span doesn't even take into account exceptional students. Since typical students differ so much developmentally, it's reasonable to expect that their rates of learning may vary significantly. If we emphasize levels of achievement, we will necessarily create competitive environments in which some students will be winners and others will be losers. Typically, the losers will withdraw or disrupt. The inspiring teacher does everything possible to avoid this situation.

Instead of emphasizing achievement, inspiring teachers focus on the task at hand: learning. Ironically, when we stress achievement, we devalue the notion that learning is a continuous process. Students who are more concerned with outcomes can quickly develop the belief that they are "done" learning about a particular topic when, in fact, learning is a never-ending journey.

Inspiring teachers continually help their students remain focused on their job: to learn as much as they can. With that definition of the student role, there is no end to learning. Just as important, this focus is equally inviting to all students, regardless of their strengths and weaknesses. All students can do their best and learn as much as possible. When students understand their job and know they will not be compared with others, they are much more likely to become the inspired students we want them to be.

A PASSION FOR TEACHING AND LEARNING

Until now, I've emphasized the importance of human relationships in the inspiring classroom. Without those supportive relationships, I don't think we can expect large numbers of students to do quality work.

Beyond the human relationship is the relationship teachers have with their material. Each inspiring teacher is unique. Each has special talents and gifts. One thing they all share, however, is a love of learning and a passion for the subjects they teach. While enthusiasm is not necessarily contagious, boredom is deadly. Teachers who do not communicate excitement, joy in learning, and passion about what they teach can never hope to inspire. Those who inspire find many ways to communicate to learners that the subject they are studying is relevant, stimulating, able to change their lives, and worth working hard to learn.

The next time a student says, "Why would anyone want to learn this?" understand that you are probably dealing with a mismatcher who is giving you an opportunity to explain why your lifework is worthwhile. What a gift! With all your energy and enthusiasm, explain exactly why your subject matter is well worth the student's full attention, time, and effort. Answering with passion about the importance of what you teach is more inspiring than saying, "Because you need it to graduate." The issue is really quite simple: Do we want students who satisfy graduation requirements, or do we want inspired learners who are excited about the process of lifelong learning?

Making Lessons Relevant

John Shea teaches sixth grade at the Plymouth Community Intermediate School in Massachusetts. He models many of the ideas that can inspire students. In the spring of 1997, John decided to make his teaching of writing as relevant as possible by focusing on a real-life event.

A report evaluating schools across the country had just been published in Education Week. John had his students write letters to Dr. John Silber, chairman of the Massachusetts Board of Education, suggesting ways to improve schools that were rated only C in the report. When students are given a writing assignment, they sometimes ask, "Why do we have to write this?" When John asked his students to express their ideas about improving school quality to a prominent person in education, they worked hard, did their best work, and did not complain that they were being asked to do something useless or irrelevant.

In their letters, many students wrote that they believed schools would be more effective if teachers intentionally made learning fun. When Dr. Silber first read the letters, he understood students' use of the word fun in a narrow sense. In his initial letter to students in May 1997, he wrote: "It was striking to note how many of you felt that if education is not entertaining and fun, then students will not learn anything. You felt that students should learn because they wanted to, not because they had to. However, it is important to remember that we have to do many things in life, and not all of them are necessarily amusing. Entertainment in the classroom can play a valuable role, but it can also become a substitute for academic effort and hard work. In addition, it can do students a grave disservice by creating the impression that throughout their lives, someone will be there to make things fun for them. Unfortunately, that is rarely the case."

Dr. Silber's letter is interesting for several reasons. Students had written that they could learn more from doing fun activities than from sitting in class doing worksheets and reading from textbooks. Dr. Silber's opening sentence distorts their comments. His second sentence suggests that he is unaware of the teacher's role as a lead manager in a classroom. In that role, teachers use a variety of skills to help students "want" to learn. They do not sit back passively and teach only what students want without trying to expand students' perspectives. Finally, the notion that creating a fun-filled environment may represent a "grave disservice" is curious. Extending that line of reasoning, we might reach the conclusion that inspiring teachers do their students a disservice, given that these same students may encounter less-skilled teachers along the way.

Fortunately, the students were interested in engaging in ongoing, meaningful dialogue and were not deterred by Dr. Silber's response. They took the time to write additional letters. On June 12, 1997, Dr. Silber wrote a letter to one of the students that supported what many of them had suggested: "However, no one is suggesting that students should spend hours in school reading textbooks... Good teachers know how to strike a balance between the use of textbooks with other books and the inclusion of activities, projects, and games that build upon the material being studied and enhance its understanding and retention... Have as much fun as you can have consistent with learning all that you need to learn. Work hard so that the doors of college will be open to you, and so you will be able to find a job or a profession that gives you great satisfaction at the same time that it provides the means to support a family of your own."

Despite some misunderstanding, these students were provided with one of the most meaningful learning experiences they may ever have. The efforts of a group of sixth grade students, led by an inspiring teacher, demonstrate that when we engage in honest, vigorous dialogue, it is possible to learn from one another and develop new, more constructive perceptions.

Create Your Own Homework

Teachers John Shea and Mary Madden from the Plymouth Community Intermediate School, along with Ann Best Shea, an elementary teacher at Forestdale School in Sandwich, Massachusetts, have developed a strategy they call "Create Your Own Homework." Frustrated because too many students did not complete homework regularly or did the work but ended up disliking school and learning, these teachers devised a way to make homework useful, relevant, and something that inspired students to want to become lifelong learners.

"Create Your Own Homework" balances freedom and structure. Students complete a homework project each week. The nature of that project is where students are given freedom. Since these inspiring teachers are interested in having students develop good study habits, the topics students choose are not particularly important. The teachers do, however, provide students with suggested categories each week to encourage varied learning activities, such as writing, reading, analyzing data, and doing calculations. After students have finished their homework assignments, they fill out a self-evaluation form, providing information about what they learned, how long they worked, and how they can demonstrate their learning to peers. By engaging in this self-evaluation process, students have a structured opportunity to think about what type of learning they have been involved in and how their new knowledge might be applied.

Each Friday, students in John and Mary's classroom have some time to present the results of their week's work. So many students want to share what they have learned that the teachers have developed a sign-up system. There is never a shortage of volunteers, and virtually all the students in the class, including those with identified special education needs, proudly present their work to their teachers and classmates.

What do parents think about this departure from the traditional homework routine? Most are both supportive and grateful. They see their children completing homework assignments with enthusiasm, sometimes for the first time ever. Parents are delighted that their children actively seek information and eagerly do more than is required because they are experiencing the joy of learning. "Create Your Own Homework" is a highly effective technique designed to inspire quality. To many parents, it seems like a miracle.

Teaching Literature

If you teach literature—or, for that matter, any other discipline involving human interaction—it's easy to build the principles of choice theory and brain-based learning into your learning plans. Some years ago, a teacher asked me to help out in her eighth grade English classroom. She was interested in teaching her students some important choice theory concepts but wanted them to flow naturally from her English lessons. Although she thought choice theory was important, she didn't want to teach it separately at the expense of her primary role as an English teacher. She invited me to visit her class for a day.

I spent a few minutes with the students discussing and defining what I meant by the terms responsibility and responsible behaviors. We all agreed that responsible behavior means acting in a way that satisfies our needs without interfering with others' attempts to satisfy theirs. It is also behavior that is safe and legal. I then briefly outlined the four psychological basic needs choice theory suggests: love/belonging, power, freedom, and fun. The entire teaching component took no more than 15 minutes.

The students were reading *The Pigman* by Paul Zindel. The day before I visited their class, they had read the first half of the novel. Together, we listed the behaviors that the three main characters had already engaged in. Then, the students broke into learning teams. Their task was to discuss what need or needs the behaviors had satisfied. (Remember, all our behavior is purposeful and is intended to satisfy our basic needs). One of the most gratifying outcomes of the lesson was listening as the students argued about what need a given behavior addressed. I then asked the students whether the behaviors would be better classified as "responsible" or "less responsible." I also asked the learning teams to have some reasons for their decisions. What followed was a lively discussion about motivation and responsibility.

The teacher did not need me to return for the follow-up lesson. She knew what she wanted to do next: examine the characters' behaviors during the second half of the novel and see whether they had grown in terms of how responsibly they acted.

In any discipline involving human interaction, it is easy to help students relate behaviors to basic needs. When appropriate, inspiring teachers can highlight the concept of responsibility, as the English teacher and I did during this discussion of *The Pigman.*

BEYOND CLIQUES: THE CARING COMMUNITY OF LEARNERS

We are social beings. The need for belonging leads us to seek the companionship of others. The need for security frequently expresses itself in our shutting others out. As a result, it is common for any group of people to be made up of a number of disconnected subgroups. Individuals feel secure within a particular group but may hesitate to make connections outside it.

In classrooms, this behavior is evident when cliques form. By their very nature, cliques are need-satisfying, addressing the needs for belonging and security. In many communities, cliques are also arenas where the need for power is expressed, frequently in irresponsible ways. Many gangs threaten or engage in violent acts, providing members with tremendous power.

Inspiring teachers address these realities. They do not pretend that the classroom doesn't have cliques or gangs. Instead, they return relentlessly to the mission of education: to have students learn as much as possible and develop skills that will help them live productive lives and make a contribution to their community. As long as that vision is inclusive, nearly every student will begin to see the value of school. Because we all have a need to be competent, all students are interested in learning how to develop skills that will give them positive recognition within their community. If we are unable to provide that recognition in our schools, we risk the chaos and violence that gangs can bring.

Inspiring teachers work with their students to develop a shared quality world vision regarding their classroom community. Students do not create this vision on their own. Young people may lack the skills necessary to envision an inclusive, inviting community of learners. Inspiring teachers have a responsibility to participate in forming the shared vision. They must make certain that all students are included in the vision, even those unable to express themselves effectively. Inspiring teachers help students understand that they are more powerful and better off when everyone in the class is fully involved and positively connected with one another. Of course, some students will naturally be more attracted to some and less attracted to others. Such behavior is human nature and should be expected and respected. Still, students have opportunities to discover that breaking down barriers of cliques and gangs helps each of them achieve more success and experience more genuine satisfaction in their class.

Not all students will accept that cooperating and creating a caring community is worthwhile or even desirable. Some will be so frightened of moving outside their own comfortable group that they may resist and ridicule your efforts, at least initially. Further, bravado may mask their fear. Even when classroom situations become difficult, inspiring teachers do not give up easily. They know that they can inspire students in large numbers only when they have built a group that transcends the subgroups within the class. That knowledge sustains them during difficult times and helps them discover the resources they need to forge a genuine community from a collection of individuals and subgroups.

In creating a classroom community, inspiring teachers never challenge the value of the groups to which students already belong. They don't try to break up cliques. Instead, they help students develop a new quality world picture that incorporates the whole class. Once students leave the class, they may naturally drift back to their original cliques, where they find the safety, security, belonging, and perhaps power they seek. All those needs, however, can be satisfied within the inspiring classroom if students become positively connected to the whole class. When teachers help students discover that important fact, they begin creating a supportive, caring community of learners with relative ease.

SUMMARY

Inspiring teachers develop learning environments in which large numbers of students regularly produce quality work. The first and most important step teachers take in this process is intentionally creating positive working relationships with all of the students. They help students see themselves as members of a learning community. A positive learning environment is not an end in itself. Rather, it is in this environment that students will do their best work.

Inspiring teachers work collaboratively with their students to clarify roles and responsibilities in the classroom. They provide relevant and meaningful learning opportunities and help students appreciate why giving their best effort will benefit them. Inspiring teachers also help their students develop a vision of a quality classroom, knowing that this vision will motivate students to achieve academically and behave responsibly.

Inspiring teachers use strategies that promote high achievement, such as well-structured cooperative learning groups. They make certain that all students, even those frequently misunderstood, are valued and included in the learning community. Fueled by a love of learning and a passion for the subjects they teach, inspiring teachers help make their classrooms exciting places where students are encouraged to explore, challenge themselves, and grow both academically and socially.

CHAPTER 6

Inspiring Your Colleagues

Throughout this book, we explore how teachers can inspire their students. Many teachers also want to know whether they can influence their colleagues. This chapter suggests ways that teachers can inspire their colleagues and move from isolated efforts toward systemic change.

DON'T PREACH

When I conduct workshops to help teachers and schools increase quality, participants frequently ask how they can influence their colleagues and begin putting some of these ideas into practice schoolwide. Their language often reveals just how much they have internalized the belief system inherent in external control psychology. They ask how they can "make" their colleagues see the value of the ideas, not realizing that they, too, are operating from a coercive, external control perspective. They talk about how everyone "should" believe what they now believe, unaware that their language denies their colleagues the opportunity to evaluate the ideas for themselves. Most disturbing, some speak with the overzealousness of having just discovered the truth—and they're obliged to share it with everyone else whether or not a person wants to hear it.

I am pleased when other professionals find my workshops valuable. Nevertheless, when they are too enthusiastic, I encourage them to slow down and not destroy relationships with colleagues who may not know what they know and may not believe what they believe. Most of us lack patience with colleagues who preach to us after they have had a particularly meaningful learning experience. The preacher who gives unsolicited advice has forgotten some important concepts: all of us are doing the best we can, all behavior is purposeful, and people do what makes good sense to them even if you believe you have learned a better way to do things. Unsolicited advice is the thinly disguised twin of criticism, the most destructive behavior we can use with others.

If you want to ensure that your colleagues will never move in your direction, preach to them. Tell them you have found the truth and now know how to inspire students. It won't take long for you to become an outcast in your building, largely ignored and certainly not appreciated. You may have wonderful information, but unless you present yourself less offensively, your information will be rendered useless. No one will listen to what you've got to say. How, then, can you influence your colleagues?

WALK THE TALK

If you want to influence your colleagues, your actions must be congruent with your words. Model the principles that inspire others. Create an inviting, nonjudgmental environment with your colleagues. Do not offer advice unless asked. Go about your business and build genuine relationships with your colleagues. Remember that we are multidimensional beings with lives that extend beyond the school and the world of education.

Just as inspiring teachers show genuine interest in their

students, teachers who wish to inspire their colleagues demonstrate genuine interest in them. They communicate with colleagues about the stuff of ordinary experience, such as family, hobbies, weekend plans, vacations, illness, interests, and current events. If you only talk to colleagues about school and school-related issues, you don't really know them. You only know a part of them, albeit an important part. If you and your colleagues have a more complete connection, one that is both genuine and respectful of the privacy each person wishes to maintain, your colleagues will more likely talk with you about issues that matter, including school.

PRESERVING INDIVIDUAL STYLE

Some wonderful teachers or teachers in training reading my ideas on how to become an inspiring teacher might feel excluded. The language I use might be characterized as nurturing or even too soft. I talk about "inviting" students to "embrace" what we are "offering." I emphasize the importance of offering students "choice." I suggest that teachers intentionally provide "learning plans" that are "relevant" and "useful" to students. I say that inspiring teachers are "never" interested in "punishment," only in teaching a more responsible set of behaviors. I speak about the destructive nature of "criticism," even "constructive criticism." Finally, I even suggest that "learning" is more important than "achievement."

There is no one way of being an inspiring teacher. Inspiring teachers present themselves in many different ways. Here's the story of an inspiring teacher who exemplifies how personal styles can vary.

Dave Driscoll is a former marine. A large man with a booming voice, he has a presence that can intimidate adults and students alike. Dave organizes his elementary classes in a no-nonsense way that is more dictatorship than democracy. Through both Dave's reputation and direct experience, students learn that his classroom is a place where hard work is expected and disrupting the learning is to be avoided.

Most important, Dave Driscoll is an inspiring teacher. What qualities does Dave bring to the classroom that inspire students? Above all else, he brings a passion for learning. When students enter his classroom, they are bombarded with information. Learning is the objective, and the sources of inspiration are many and varied. There is a reference section in the room. There are computers, many borrowed from colleagues who have not taken the time to learn how to effectively incorporate them into the curriculum. There is Internet access, allowing students to have the most current information from around the world at their fingertips. There are posters around the room. Some are inspirational, filled with quotations about hard work, achievement, and the joy of persevering. Some are content related, providing information about an array of topics. In any classroom, no matter how inspiring the teacher and how relevant the subject matter, students will drift and eyes will wander. In Dave's classroom, drifting eyes encounter something worth learning.

My son, Greg, was fortunate enough to learn from Dave. So far, Greg has been a high-achieving student. He also has the capacity to be disruptive, though not maliciously. It would be inaccurate to say that Greg never disrupted Dave's sixth grade class, but the disruptions were infrequent and easily managed, and the learning was of the highest quality.

I asked Greg what he valued most about Dave Driscoll. "Mr. Driscoll can be tough, but he's always fair," Greg told me. I remember one experience in particular where Dave combined firmness, fairness, and reason to enhance Greg's learning.

Dave had given the students a math test to work on over several days. He encouraged students to work at home and use whatever resources they had to solve the problems. Greg had never found it necessary to write down assignments. His memory had been adequate, and he saw no reason to put something in writing when he could easily remember what and when something was due.

Greg worked diligently on his math test. He submitted it on the morning he thought it was due, confident that he had done well. Dave asked him if he wanted it corrected, a question he did not ordinarily ask.

"Sure," Greg answered. "Why do you ask?"

"I was just curious," Dave said. "Since you didn't turn it in on time, you won't receive any credit. I just wanted to know if you were still interested in my feedback."

To some, this response may sound harsh and punitive. I, too, think the inflexibility was unnecessary, but the most important perception is the student's. When I asked Greg what he thought, he was quick to tell me that Mr. Driscoll treats all students equally. Greg said he was aware of the consequences for not turning in work on time. In his mind, the response was fair.

When I spoke with Dave about the situation, he asked me whether I was comfortable with how he managed it. I told him that I only had one important question: What effect would this episode have on Greg's placement in the coming school year? Dave assured me that something of this nature would never adversely affect a student's academic placement.

In addition to possessing a passion for teaching and a profound sense of fairness, Dave follows the principles of brain-based learning in his classroom. He adapts his teaching approach to what current research suggests is most effective. Since knowledge about particular topics increases so rapidly today, Dave makes great use of the most current technology, including the Internet. Textbooks are secondary in his classroom. They are resources that aid the teacher, not the masters that drive the teaching. Finally, Dave has a clear sense of what he wants students to be able to do at the completion of a lesson or unit. He provides them with freedom and options in terms of how they master the material. His primary goals are that they master the material and demonstrate competence.

Inspiring teachers are not cut from the same mold. Some can be demanding and at times rigidly harsh. If you hope to inspire, your individuality and creativity must shine through.

Many of us have had special teachers during our lives, people who inspired us. Dave Driscoll was one of those teachers for my son and for many other students in our community. I am grateful that my son had a chance to be inspired by this special teacher.

CREATING AND SUSTAINING ENERGY IN YOUR BUILDING

An inspiring teacher can operate independently within any school or district. In fact, many inspiring teachers have been working in isolation for years. That situation can be lonely. When you are inspiring students, creating need-satisfying classrooms, and building brain-friendly learning environments, you naturally want to share your success with others and have others available to help you during difficult times.

A school becomes a more exciting place to work when you are one of many working intentionally to inspire others. Aren't all teachers working to inspire students? I don't believe so. Even if they are, their efforts are not necessarily as focused and intentional as they might be. There is a subtle but profound difference between teachers who are doing the best they can and teachers who are mindful of their capacity to inspire large numbers of students.

If you are one of several people working intentionally to inspire students in your building or district, consider forming some type of networking group. (In many areas, these efforts bring credits for professional development.) A networking group builds and sustains energy. Except for a few exceptional teachers, working in isolation is exhausting and ultimately unsatisfactory. For most, being connected to a larger group committed to the same ideas sustains them.

Within a networking group, teachers share strategies and successes. To keep from being a destructive force within the school community, your group should avoid negative comments and open regular "energizing and inspiring" meetings to all staff members. If membership is restricted, you will be modeling elitism, clique building, and divisiveness. Be careful not to be exclusive and uninviting in covert ways. For example, when new members attend a meeting, notice whether you refer to discussions that occurred before the new members were present. If so, you give the loud nonverbal message that although all staff members can come to meetings, you're going to discuss things that don't involve them and create an atmosphere where they feel excluded. Under those conditions, some may drop in for a session, but your core group will remain a small band of elitists who do little to change the school's culture.

Changing the culture of a school, even a school that is already a great place to teach and learn, is one of the things inspiring teachers may try to do. They help make struggling schools successful and successful schools even better. No matter how effective any individual teacher is, it takes a critical mass of people to initiate cultural change. That's the power of starting a networking group of interested teachers. Collective action gives you the potential to inspire on a larger scale.

Who begins a networking group? Most of us are so stuck in the thinking of external control psychology that we immediately answer, "Someone else." We may see it as the function of administration. I agree that administrators have a role to play. If we want to take more effective control of our professional lives, however, we will no longer wait for someone else to begin what we believe is worthwhile. While we should not proceed impulsively or circumvent established chains of command, we should take responsibility by taking responsible action.

How do you create your networking group? Begin by figuring out whether any other staff are interested in forming a discussion group on how to grow professionally and inspire more students to work hard in school. There is interest in most schools. Many schools are full of latent energy waiting to be tapped.

Teachers are reluctant to give precious time to anything that has no value. You need to help your colleagues realize that what you are suggesting will add quality to their lives. What does that mean? First, teachers, especially experienced teachers, will want to know how the group will be different from any of the education fads they may have encountered. Otherwise, they will devote their time to more meaningful pursuits. You can assure them that what they are becoming involved in has the potential to make a difference for their students. Second, point out that moving in a direction that inspires more students to work harder and excel academically will make their jobs more enjoyable. Some may be moved by comments about improved quality in education. All, however, will be interested in learning about how to enjoy their jobs more.

It is essential to get administrative approval for a formal networking effort. The ideal group has active administrative leadership, not simply approval. Waiting for such leadership, however, keeps you passive. You are relying on someone else in order to experience satisfaction. Appreciate what others can do for you, but don't give up being proactive while others decide how they want to proceed. Strong administrative leadership is desirable. Nevertheless, move forward once there is administrative approval for a networking group to begin meeting regularly in the building.

Are administrators likely to approve a group of this nature? That depends largely on what exactly you present to them for consideration. Any reasonable administrator would encourage the staff to discuss ways to help more students consistently work harder and do better work. Any reasonable administrator would encourage staff to discuss current brain research about how people learn most effectively. Any reasonable administrator would encourage staff to share successes and proven strategies so that collective wisdom is fully used and the culture of the school supports student growth and learning. If you present these ideas wisely, the administrator will likely approve them—and perhaps even offer enthusiastic support.

HOW DO WE COMMUNICATE?

Diane Gossen and Judy Anderson (1995) have identified three types of schools. The conventional school is the traditional school where teachers are relatively autonomous and work in isolation. There is little or no sharing in this school. Teachers tend to keep their doors closed and maintain a level of competition with each other.

The congenial school is characterized by friendships, celebrations, and other social events. Because the emphasis is on getting along with others, teachers in the congenial school spend a lot of energy avoiding conflict. Keeping the peace is valued most, so potentially conflict-laden topics are avoided. When they are brought up, many remain silent, although silent meetings are often followed by vibrant gossip sessions. M. Scott Peck (1988, 109) identifies this social structure as a "pseudocommunity." Its members display the fear-driven belief that honest disagreement and conflict will undermine valued relationships.

The collegial school is not afraid of conflict. In this setting, vigorous dialogue and all the attending conflict are regularly engaged in. Staff believe that relationships are strengthened when they engage in honest, quality interactions instead of settling for superficiality in both dialogue and relationships. They know that superficiality is an enemy of quality, including quality relationships. A thorough understanding of choice theory psychology can be a significant factor in helping staff move to this level of interaction.

Inspiring teachers help move their schools toward becoming collegial schools. They respect differences and argue respectfully, but they passionately engage in discussions about how to make classrooms and schools even better. From my discussions about these concepts with teachers around the country, I believe we are making steady progress away from conventional schools. Teachers are sharing more with one another and working in less isolation. Most tell me, however, that their schools are much more congenial than collegial. To achieve meaningful school improvement, inspiring teachers take steps to create truly collegial schools, the most professional environment in which to conduct the important work of education.

MAKING CONNECTIONS BEYOND YOUR BUILDING

Inspiring teachers can build and maintain energy by connecting with others outside their buildings or systems. Even if you feel isolated within your building because others are not intentionally working toward the same goals, it can be comforting to know that many others around the country and the world are engaged in the same pursuit as you.

You can network in many ways with others outside your school. You might find it useful to attend workshops and conferences and to join organizations specifically formed to improve schools and inspire students. These outside contacts allow you to continue your learning while simultaneously receiving validation that you are moving in a positive direction. The bibliography provides some Web sites to help you begin your search for other professionals striving to inspire quality.

It would be wonderful if your colleagues appreciated all the innovative, effective ideas that are available. Inspiring teachers, though, are not so patient that they will wait for others. All are invited to journey together, but inspiring teachers are moving ahead now.

THE IMPORTANCE OF ADMINISTRATIVE LEADERSHIP

I would like to believe that inspiring teachers are so competent that they can be successful even without strong leadership from administration. They still can inspire their students even when faced with a relatively hostile environment and an unenlightened administrator. Inspiring teachers have been doing that for years. To make significant gains in the culture of the school, however, inspiring teachers need strong leadership from building-level administrators.

If you work in a building that does not yet have supportive leadership, you have several options. One is simply to accept the situation as it is and do what you can within your particular classroom. As long as you genuinely get satisfaction from what you are doing and accept that you inspire your students but don't influence change on a larger scale, this option is perfectly legitimate.

If you want your influence to extend beyond the door of your classroom, other options exist. Begin the process of engaging the administration. The same qualities that help you to inspire your students will help you in this process. You first need to build a healthy involvement and positive working relationship with administration. This is one area where many inspiring teachers are woefully deficient. Adept at forging strong working relationships with reluctant students, they have great difficulty doing the same with reluctant administrators. Many get caught in the "they're adults and administrators, so they should know better" trap. Such thoughts may be true, but they do nothing to improve the relationships or the school. Keep remembering this: all of us, including less-enlightened colleagues and administrators, are doing the best we can. If you believe you have something valuable to offer administrators, if you hope to inspire them, begin forging positive working relationships. Anything less is likely to be counterproductive. Contrary to what you might think, some administrators really do want to lead with energy, enthusiasm, and vision, but they may lack the skills and the courage. Everyone can benefit if you let your administrators know that you truly want them to lead you on a journey that will make your school an even better place to grow and learn.

Another option--one not to be exercised without considerable thought--is to move to another school system. More schools are moving toward increased quality, and more administrators are actively leading their staffs on an exciting journey. The idea of moving may be frightening, but for some it is the right thing to do. Again, any major career decision should be undertaken only after serious reflection. For some, a move represents their best chance to inspire more colleagues and more students.

SUMMARY

Many inspiring teachers want to reach out to their colleagues. The most helpful first step in this process is to model what you espouse. Over time, some of your colleagues will indicate an interest in how they, too, can be more satisfied in their work and more successful with their students. As an increasing number of teachers intentionally work to inspire students to do quality work consistently, professionals can share ideas and support one another. With active leadership from administrators, inspiring teachers can collectively create the cultural shift necessary to initiate long-lasting systemic change.

CHAPTER 7

Forging an Alliance with Parents

Parents are one of a school's most valuable and least valued resources. Today, more and more parents are frustrated by public schools and public school teachers. As a result, increasing numbers of students are being enrolled in private schools or are being home educated. Charter schools—public schools funded with taxpayers' money but unencumbered by many of the rules governing traditional public schools—are gaining popularity.

I find these trends alarming. Public education is a cornerstone of a democratic society. If the public continues turning to alternative forms of education, we will compromise the fundamental principle that we as a society will provide the resources to educate our children. We will be systematically creating a distinct class system. Parents who have the financial resources will understandably give their children an educational experience different from that of the traditional public school. Their children will have a distinct advantage over children in public schools when it's time to apply to college or for jobs. Pay and other markers of respect will go disproportionately to a smaller elite, and our grand democratic experiment will end.

My words are not meant as hyperbole. I truly believe we need a public school system that provides a quality education for the vast majority in order for our form of government to work. A small minority will always be educated separately and provided with advantages unavailable to the masses. As long as their numbers remain small, we continue to function with a reasonably effective democracy. I fear, however, that the numbers are growing and that our social structure may be significantly altered if we do not take effective action quickly.

We need to reengage parents who have lost faith in public education and public educators. If we want to bring parents back, we must find ways to help them appreciate that we know what we are doing and that their children will get a quality educational experience in our schools.

WHAT WENT WRONG?

Instead of blaming others for the current adversarial relationship that exists between too many parents and educators, inspiring teachers prefer to look in the mirror and ask, "What went wrong? Why is it that so many parents don't trust us, think that we are ill-prepared to teach their children, and turn in desperation to educational alternatives?" In answering these questions, it is not important whether the perceptions of parents are accurate. If parents believe that public educators are less committed and competent than teachers in other settings, they will act on the basis of that perception. One goal of inspiring teachers, therefore, is to create a strong working alliance with parents that is characterized by mutual respect and support.
Understanding that the only behavior they can control is their own, inspiring teachers take immediate action to create the conditions that will lead to a positive alliance with parents. They don't wait for parents to make the first move.

INTIMIDATION

Too many parents are intimidated by schools, teachers, and a system they don't fully understand. Often, school staff contact parents only when there is a problem. Although this situation can occur at any level, it is especially common in secondary schools. Secondary teachers have large numbers of students and find it difficult to have regular, positive contact with parents. When a student is doing poorly, however, teachers almost always contact parents.

When most parents are contacted by the school, they wonder, What's wrong? They are likely to be defensive and cautious, decreasing the chances of establishing a strong, cooperative working relationship. If we help parents perceive school-initiated contact less negatively, we would be much better off.

Why do parents typically jump to the "there must be something wrong if the school is contacting me" perception? Because that too often has been their experience. Think of all the calls you have made as a professional to the homes of your students. Were most of these calls made because of problems, or were you just as likely to call when things were going well?

Most teachers tell me that their calls primarily fall in the negative category. They are quick to justify their behavior, often explaining that they have too many students and not enough time. I know they are doing the best they can, and their explanations may be valid. To move toward building good relationships with parents, however, teachers must address these important questions: What type of relationship do you want to have with parents? How do you want parents to perceive you and the school? Is the way you are currently behaving toward parents—for example, only calling them when there is a problem—helping you get what you want? We are all busy. Don't let that truth prevent you from evaluating how effectively your behavior is helping you achieve positive, supportive relationships with parents.

If you conclude that your way of contacting parents has been less helpful to you, what can you do? There are a number of ways to begin remedying the situation. I will offer a couple of ideas to get you started. I hesitate to offer too many because inspiring teachers are usually better off coming up with their own solutions. I hope you will tailor my suggestions to suit your needs and your style and will add your own creative ideas.

Some teachers regularly make positive phone contacts with all the parents of their students. To keep the conversations manageable, they let parents know they have only a few minutes to talk, but they make it clear that they want to develop a positive working relationship. The tone of each conversation is both professional and light, and the focus is on developing the quality world vision that both the teacher and the parents want the child to be a successful student. Together, the teacher and the parents begin discussing how they can act toward each other as two important adult influences in the child's life.

It's hard to overstate the value of such conversations. Parents usually so appreciate your taking the time to contact them simply because you want their child to experience success that they will support you as the year unfolds. If you must contact them later because of a problem, the positive history you have already established will help you work collaboratively. Instead of behaving defensively, the parents will more likely be motivated to work things out.

Secondary teachers may have student loads that make phone contact with each parent cumbersome. Inspiring teachers have developed creative ways to manage this situation. When students are grouped into teams, for example, each team's teachers can share the responsibility of contacting parents. During their conversations, teachers are clear that they are speaking not only for themselves but for all the team's teachers and that they all want to work successfully with parents.

If phone conversations are too time consuming for you, a letter to parents may be helpful. Remember that the purpose of the letter is to engage parents and build an alliance. Refrain from including anything extraneous. Write with forging a partnership in mind. Personalize your letter as much as possible. Personalized letters to parents clearly communicate that you have taken some time for them as individuals. The powerful message that you care about them and their child will never hurt your relationship, and it has the potential to help it significantly.

Besides phone contacts from school staff, school meetings often intimidate parents. I have attended numerous meetings that included 6 to 10 professional educators and only a single parent. Imagine what that must feel like to the parent, especially considering that school meetings often take place because of some difficulty a student is experiencing. The parent sits alone in a room full of professionals who are in a familiar environment and among colleagues. Like all of us, parents have a need for power, a need to feel competent. In this situation, the parent probably feels incompetent and responds in any number of ways to protect against that discomfort. Some blame and criticize the teachers. Some berate their child in an effort to develop an alliance with the teachers. Some sit silently, almost numb, waiting only for the meeting to end. Regardless, it's hard to imagine a successful conference under these circumstances.

How, then, can meetings be made less intimidating and more inviting for parents? First, limit the number of people at the meeting. Second, include at least one staff member with whom the parent has a positive, trusting connection. Third, the person who chairs the meeting should articulate the objective: to help the student be more successful in school. Any comments that can move the group in that direction are welcome. Anything that has little value, including blaming and arguing, is discouraged.

Some schools designate a staff member on a rotating basis to "play the parent" at meetings. This person listens to comments from the likely perspective of the parent. The staff member asks questions that a timid parent might fear asking or that an uninformed parent might not think to ask. This procedure assures that important parental viewpoints are discussed regardless of the actual parent's behavior.

Inspiring teachers ask, "How can we behave so that each parent will feel less intimidated and more willing to create a partnership with us for the benefit of the student?" As they answer, individually or in concert with other teachers, they discover ways to move in a more positive direction.

FEAR

Fear is one of the most significant barriers to quality. When we feel fear, we automatically revert to more primitive behaviors designed to protect us. The brain shifts into a survival mode (Howard 1994, 259). Blood rushes to the large muscles, those most helpful when the appropriate choice is fight or flight. Of course, if most of the oxygenated blood is rushing to the large muscles, another part of the body suffers a decrease in blood, oxygen, and other nutrients: the brain. Specifically, the brain's frontal lobes, the end point in the circulation route, suffer first and most when we feel threatened. The frontal lobes are responsible for long-range thinking, problem solving, and higher-level thinking skills.

If we desire productive meetings with parents, a fear-laden environment is counterproductive. Despite our best intent, too many parents still fear us because of their own school experiences, and they bring their fear into meetings with us. Knowing this, inspiring teachers do everything possible to minimize fear in dealing with others at all times. Our words can be a helpful starting point, but they must be backed by action if we want parents to believe us. It is not enough to say, "We understand this meeting must be hard for you, especially discussing your child's difficulty in school. We want to work cooperatively with you so that your child can be a successful student." Parents must leave the meeting believing that we really did work cooperatively for the benefit of their child if they are ever to trust us, or any school personnel, again. We must choose our words carefully, mean what we say, and deliver on any promises that we make. Over time, as we earn a reputation as people who mean what we say and who truly work with parents for the betterment of students, parents will trust us more and fear us less.

CONDESCENDING BEHAVIORS

At the beginning of my workshops, I ask teachers to identify behaviors that they find bothersome in a workshop leader. They usually say, "Don't be condescending. We dislike it when someone talks down to us. If you do that to us, we'll turn you off."

Parents are no different from teachers. When we talk down to them and belittle them, they turn us off. We lose any chance of providing them with important information and building an alliance with them.

There are many ways to be condescending. Some professionals enjoy using specialized terminology that confuses anyone outside the field. Sometimes the condescending behaviors are more subtle, involving tone of voice, body language, and when and how people are acknowledged. To determine whether your approach is condescending, ask, "If I were the parent at this meeting, would I feel like a valued member of the team, someone who is respected as much as everyone else at the table, or would I feel trivialized, patronized, and 'put up with' because I am viewed as someone who must be tolerated but not respected?" The answer will help you figure out what you need to do next.

"THESE PARENTS DON'T CARE"

One of the least helpful comments we can make is "These parents don't care." First, it is an assumption, not a verifiable truth. Second, in nearly every case, it is patently absurd. In 25 years of working in public education, I have encountered many parents who had horribly deficient parenting skills, but I have not met one about whom I would say, "This parent doesn't care."

Those of us who are parents know from experience just how erroneous such a statement is. Even those who are not parents can probably imagine what it is like to be a parent. Whether we are talking about effective parents or ineffective parents, well-educated parents or less-well-educated parents, economically well-off parents or economically disadvantaged parents, couples or single parents, all of them want their children to be successful. They may not be skilled enough to demonstrate their desire clearly, or we may not be skilled enough to identify it, but parents do care about their children.

Inspiring teachers ask, "Does it help me to see some parents as uncaring? Would it be more helpful and just as reasonable to see parents as caring but unskilled in some way or uninformed about something I think is important?" The latter approach allows you to view parents more favorably, work more comfortably with them, and clarify your role—which is to provide additional skills or information that will help them become more effective parents.

"PARENTS THINK THEY ARE EDUCATIONAL EXPERTS"

Many parents believe they are knowledgeable about the field of education because they have attended school. Unlike education, most other professions are more self-contained and isolated. Few patients believe they know enough about medicine to question their doctors. Legal clients trust that their attorneys know more about law than they do.

Teachers often complain about parents who are poorly informed but richly opinionated. These parents have little or no knowledge about what educators know to be the best current practices. They have little or no information about the latest research. Still, they cling to a belief that they know a lot by virtue of having spent considerable time in school.

Inspiring teachers are able to interact effectively with these parents. Understanding that people are internally driven and that the behavior and attitudes of parents don't control anyone, inspiring teachers choose behaviors that work best with these parents. They stay focused on their goal: to build and maintain a positive working relationship. The parents can be acknowledged as caring and concerned. Identifying areas of agreement with parents and forging a shared quality world vision is far more effective than criticizing them.

Once a positive relationship has been established, parents are more receptive to what inspiring teachers have to say. Because they have established their credibility, inspiring teachers are trusted even by opinionated parents, and they can provide them with information that will change their perceptions about teachers and education. Specifically, inspiring teachers help parents appreciate how difficult and complex teaching is. They explain to parents how much more we know today about how people learn and what types of learning environments are most academically valid.

The most opinionated and vocal parents have the potential to become our biggest allies because they're so energetic and passionate about their children's education. Our job is to educate them so that they voice their opinions loudly in support of what we are doing. Until we find a way to develop positive relationships with these parents, they will remain formidable adversaries rather than valuable allies.

"PARENTS DON'T SUPPORT US"

A common charge among educators is that parents and the community don't support them. The lack of support is especially felt when voters decide not to provide the funding sought for maintaining or enhancing programs.

It's easy to criticize and blame an unsupportive community and wallow in collective frustration and anger. Inspiring teachers, however, ask, "What have we done or failed to do that has led to a lack of support from parents and the community?" They realize that, in most cases, the lack of support is a result of poor relationships with parents and the community. They accept that they have been unsuccessful in communicating to taxpayers why spending money on education is important. Instead of remaining mired in an unproductive cycle of complaining, inspiring teachers look for ways to engage the public. To gain greater support, they work at forging an alliance with their community and building better relationships.

I usually avoid making analogies between education and business because what occurs in schools is very different from what occurs in commercial enterprises. In this case, though, a business comparison may be helpful. Parents and the voting community represent our customers. Would any business be successful if it treated customers with as little regard as we sometimes treat parents and the community?

At times, we forget who funds us. We owe taxpayers respect and courtesy. If we have alienated, we can also engage. The choice is ours.

IDENTIFYING THE SHARED QUALITY WORLD VISION

To work successfully with parents, it is necessary to develop a shared quality world vision. Since people are motivated by whatever picture they have of their quality world, successful relationships are based upon the ability of parties to develop shared pictures. Parents may not be aware of this important truth, but inspiring teachers understand it and use it to build positive, collaborative relationships with parents.

It is easy to work effectively with parents if you stay focused on everyone's primary goal: more successful, productive students. Although you may disagree with parents about many things, this fundamental area of agreement can be the foundation for building an effective partnership. With this shared vision of successful, productive students, you can work through most other difficulties. Without it, it is virtually impossible to sustain a successful relationship.

There is nothing particularly difficult about bringing this shared quality world picture into focus. From the beginning, inspiring teachers are straightforward and articulate with parents about wanting all students to be a successful and productive. They explain that this vision motivates them and their behavior toward students and parents. Once parents understand that inspiring teachers only want what the parents want, working collaboratively becomes relatively easy. Parents become much less distrustful, aggressive, and suspicious and more supportive. There may be disagreement about specifics, but those are easily managed provided it has been established that both parties want the same thing.

When you are developing a shared quality world vision with parents, it is important to consider the perceptions of the students. While it is helpful for students to see parents and teachers working together, it is crucial that students believe that parents and teachers are working together for the students' benefit. Remember that the reason for creating an alliance with parents is to benefit the students. If students believe that adults have joined forces against them, the results will be disastrous. Students will feel powerless and will likely find ways to sabotage whatever efforts parents and teachers make.

"YOU KNOW YOUR CHILD BEST"

All of us work best in need-satisfying environments. When parents believe that teachers sincerely seek and use their input, they feel valued, and the teacher-parent relationship improves. They will offer greater support to teachers, and teachers can be more effective in the classroom. Many inspiring teachers find it helpful to ask parents for such information as how their children learn best and what strategies are most and least successful. A letter or questionnaire sent home at the beginning of the school year can help in this regard.

It is just as helpful to ask students for their input. How do they learn best? What strategies work best for them? Again, if we communicate solely with parents and don't directly involve students, many students will feel powerless and disconnected.

VISITORS ARE WELCOME

Many parents feel unwelcome in schools. They often get the impression that teachers don't want to see them. These parents behave in several ways. They may become less connected to their schools generally and provide less direct support to their children on academic issues. They may speak negatively about their schools, showing their children that it is acceptable to treat teachers with disrespect. Finally, they may fail to support schools financially. Besides affecting teachers' paychecks, decreased funding reduces the educational resources available to students.

Inspiring teachers make it clear that parental visits are not only acceptable but encouraged. In too many schools, the only time parents visit is when there is a problem. In fact, some schools work overtly with parents to use parental visits as punishment for students. That's the kind of collaboration inspiring teachers work hard to avoid. Instead, they make classroom visits by parents commonplace. When parents are a regular part of the landscape, their visits are less of a distracting novelty. Students remain appropriately focused on their academic tasks.

To prevent visits from being disruptive, inspiring teachers develop appropriate guidelines, but parents still feel welcome. Many inspiring teachers find it useful to ask parents to assist in some way when they visit the classroom. This strategy has several advantages. The students feel more comfortable when a visiting adult is busy with some helpful task instead of simply observing them. The parent generally feels less awkward. In addition, the parents get a better sense of how hard teachers work, what is involved in successful teaching, and how skilled inspiring teachers are.

In a classroom that welcomes parents, you still can develop reasonable limits. It is acceptable to tell parents that they can't visit during particular days or times. You may already have another guest visiting, or you may have planned a class activity that would be disrupted by a visitor. Parents will usually understand your need to schedule visits in a way that enhances their children's educational experience.

PARENT EXPERTS IN THE CLASSROOM

Visits by parents who are experts in particular fields can enhance learning and help build strong teacher-parent relationships. It is educationally richer and more meaningful for students to meet a real archaeologist than to simply read about archaeology. Inspiring teachers let students and parents alike know that they would be delighted to have experts come to class to discuss topics being studied.

This type of visit is different from a visit on "career day." While the latter can be a worthwhile way to get parents into the building, it is an isolated event that has no connection with what is being studied. To get the full benefit of the visit, invite experts to class when it is most appropriate, not only on a designated "career day."

You can invite other experts from the community to speak to students as well. This strategy helps build a bridge between the school and the community at large. Students benefit because they can more clearly see the relevance of what they are being taught in class. Community members often appreciate the opportunity to help the school, especially in a genuinely valuable way. They also have the chance to see the exciting learning that takes place within an inspiring classroom.

USE OF VOLUNTEERS

Relationships with parents and the community at large can be strengthened when teachers invite volunteers to help them in the classroom. Classroom volunteers are among teachers' most enthusiastic supporters. They know how hard teachers work and how difficult a job teaching can be. Because they appreciate what teachers do, they are advocates for the public support of education.

For a volunteer program to work effectively, it is critical for teachers to identify exactly how volunteers can help them. Potential volunteers often shy away from becoming more involved in the school if the expectations are unclear. They are uncomfortable not knowing what they will be asked to do and whether they have the skills to be helpful. When you are recruiting volunteers, be specific about the kind of volunteer assistance you need, the time commitment, and the skills required. Some schools have found it worthwhile to provide in-service training for their volunteers. Given a clear picture of what is expected, many reluctant parents become enthusiastic and helpful volunteers.

SUMMARY

Inspiring teachers know that parents are a valuable resource for their schools. To create the kind of relationships that will help more students be successful, they intentionally work to involve parents in the educational process. They seek parents' input. They take steps to ensure that parents perceive the school as welcoming. As inspiring teachers strive to educate children, they take advantage of parents' professional expertise to enhance learning in their classrooms. They also invite parents to volunteer in the school. As a result, parents feel valued and respected. In such an environment, inspiring teachers create and maintain a positive alliance with parents, one that works for the benefit of the students.

CHAPTER 8

Conflict Management

Conflict is present in all relationships. The only way to avoid conflict is to avoid relationships. As long as you are in genuine relationships with others, there will be some things you want that they don't and some things they want that you don't. Sometimes everyone is driven by different quality world pictures. The goal in conflict management, therefore, is not to eliminate conflict, because eliminating conflict requires either ending a relationship or becoming less than fully genuine. The goal is to manage conflict in a mutually respectful, growth-enhancing way. Although the emphasis in this chapter is on managing conflict in a professional setting, the process can be applied successfully in any relationship, professional or personal.

Inspiring teachers recognize that interpersonal conflict is not a negative situation. Managed well, in fact, conflict is growth enhancing. Without the benefit of conflict, you are more likely to remain in your comfort zone, not giving yourself many opportunities to learn and grow. Conflict allows you to expand your horizons and broaden your knowledge and skills.

Effective conflict management is growth enhancing regardless of the overt outcome. If you leave the experience with your views unchanged, you understand an alternative viewpoint more fully and your own ideas have been strengthened. If you change your views because you have engaged in honest and thoughtful dialogue, you also have grown and profited. In either case, respectfully addressing a situation involving conflict leads to growth. It is interesting to me that many people will resolutely avoid conflict when effective conflict management produces positive results regardless of where it leads.

ACHIEVING A WIN/WIN RESULT

Four typical outcomes of interpersonal conflict are Win/Lose, Lose/Win, Kind of Win/Kind of Win, and Win/Win. (See F igures 8.1 – 8.4 on the following pages.)

In the first two situations, Win/Lose and Lose/Win (Figures 8.1 and 8.2), one party wins and the other loses. Unfortunately, most people resolve conflicts this way. Even the so-called winner loses in these situations. Because I am driven by a need for belonging, which involves cooperating, I still suffer when I win in a conflict with you. While my need for power may be stronger in this case, my need to cooperate is frustrated. What some might call a total victory is not totally satisfying. Because you have a need for power and achievement, you suffer when you lose. None of the effects on the loser is helpful in building a positive, healthy relationship. Since you feel less powerful in your relationship with me, you may be driven to "even the score," introducing a competitive element into our relationship that interferes with our ability to work together. Furthermore, the relationship necessarily becomes less need-satisfying. The less need-satisfying the relationship is, the less likely you will do quality work.

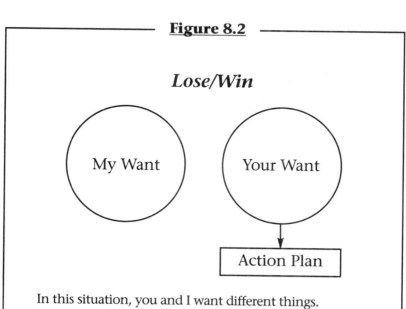

Figure 8.1

Win/Lose

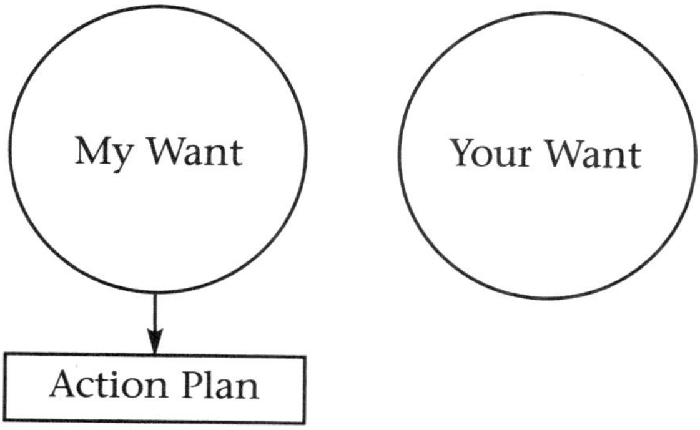

(My Want)   (Your Want)

↓

| Action Plan |

In this situation, you and I want different things.
The action plan that is developed matches what I want.
I win and you lose.

Figure 8.2

Lose/Win

(My Want)   (Your Want)

↓

| Action Plan |

In this situation, you and I want different things.
The action plan that is developed matches what you want.
You win and I lose.

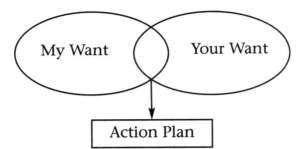

Figure 8.3

Kind of Win/Kind of Win

In this situation, the things we want partially overlap, although much of what I want is different from much of what you want. The action plan focuses on the overlapping area—each of us gets some of what we want. While this result is somewhat satisfactory, there is still much that each of us wants but doesn't get. Each of us may leave the experience feeling like a loser. We will probably be unenthusiastic when it is time to put our plan into action.

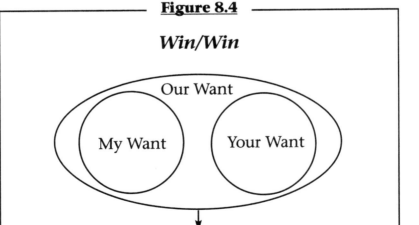

Figure 8.4

Win/Win

In this situation, the action plan incorporates what each of us wants. Both of us leave the experience feeling like winners.

If the first two results are so unsatisfactory, why do most people faced with conflict engage in behaviors that lead to them? Conflict most immediately involves the need for power. The behaviors we consider first are those designed to meet the need for power. Included in the repertoire are many competitive "power over" behaviors. Unless we have expanded our perception of power to include "power with," and unless we have developed skills to manage conflict well while maintaining a positive relationship, many of us will move quickly toward competitive "power over" behaviors, which inevitably lead to a winner and a loser. Once we have developed a more encompassing notion of power and learned the importance of belonging in and maintaining successful long-term relationships, "power over" behaviors become less attractive. We are more likely to consider alternatives that allow for the achievement of power without compromising an important relationship.

In the Kind of Win/Kind of Win situation (Figure 8.3), both parties get some of what they want. They are willing to give up a portion of their want to achieve agreement and move forward. This process is the essence of negotiation and compromise. Many who engage in negotiation and compromise—a considerable advance over the win/lose and lose/win models—do so only because they lack sufficient power in the relationship to achieve a clear-cut win. Facing the prospect of a prolonged conflict, they reluctantly begin negotiating and compromising. Keep in mind, however, that the goal in nearly every negotiation is to get as much of your want as possible while giving up as little as possible. Often in this process, there are still winners and losers, even if the victory and defeat are not complete. Those who get more of what they want and give up less to their opponents feel like winners. Those who give up more are grateful for whatever they were able to salvage of their visions, but they still feel like losers.

In many ways, the process of negotiating and compromising produces the same results as the win/lose and lose/win models. People feel less than satisfied and determined to "even the score" the next time an opportunity presents itself. Ask anyone, for example, who has ever been involved in a labor dispute that was resolved by compromise. Participants frequently leave the process feeling unsatisfied and less trustful of one another. Important working relationships are strained, if not permanently damaged. The kind of win/kind of win model may be preferable to the models with clear winners and losers, but it is far from satisfactory.

Genuine Win/Win (Figure 8.4) is the only way to manage conflict so that all parties leave feeling positive. In this model, when you and I realize that our wants do not match, we work together to develop a quality world picture that encompasses both what you want and what I want. Instead of negotiating—which involves each party trying to get the better deal—we find a solution that completely incorporates what each of us wants. Because each of us gets what we wanted to begin with, there is no compromise or giving anything up.

Behind every want are underlying needs. Sometimes it is helpful to fully explore wants to discover the underlying needs. For example, on the surface I may want a particular thing, but I come to realize that what I really need—what the want represents to me—is recognition. With that realization and an understanding that I can get just as much recognition when we develop a shared quality world picture, I easily abandon my original want and embrace the new picture. My original want is not necessarily present in the newly developed picture. Nevertheless, what it represents to me is fully captured. Because I still get my needs met, the solution represents a win/win situation.

At times, developing a shared quality world picture will be impossible. What you want and what I want will be in conflict no matter how creative we try to be or how much each of us values the other and wants to resolve a conflict. That fact does not diminish the value of beginning the conflict management process by striving for the win/win ideal. This approach is no different from inspiring teachers pursuing the ideal that every student will do quality work nearly all the time. While neither ideal can be attained regularly— that's the nature of ideals—we pursue both vigorously and accept as much success as we can reasonably expect. If we are unable to achieve a true win/win situation, we can always move to negotiation and compromise.

The conflict-management process, then, is straightforward. First, creatively pursue the development of a vision that incorporates what each party wants. If you are unable to achieve that ideal despite your best efforts, move to negotiation and compromise. The parties should treat one another respectfully and work to strengthen relationships. Poorly done negotiation and compromise can cause lasting damage. Finally, never resort to a process with clearly defined winners and losers. The cost is too high, even for those who apparently win.

WHEN CONFLICT RESOLUTION IS NOT AN OPTION

A joint effort, conflict resolution requires commitment from two or more people. Regardless of how effective any of us may be, we can only control our own behavior, not that of others. If I want to resolve a conflict and you don't, conflict resolution will not happen. When genuine conflict resolution is not an option, inspiring teachers may find it helpful to cultivate behaviors that allow them to remain centered, calm, and focused on what is most important to them.

First, remember the choice theory principle that all people are doing the best they can. It is helpful to perceive those who are unwilling to resolve conflict as doing what they know how to do instead of labeling them with such disparaging terms as "pigheaded," "stubborn," and "petty." Both perceptions are equally reasonable. Because we choose to control ourselves rather than be controlled by others, we ask, "Which perception is more helpful to maintain? Which perception will more easily allow us to act like the people we want to be?" Genuinely accepting that the other does not yet have the capacity to successfully resolve the conflict helps us stay centered, calm, and focused.

Like everyone else, you are doing the best you can. Sometimes, however, it is difficult to calmly accept another's behavior. Despite your best attempts, you remain angry, hostile, and annoyed. In such situations, the following process can be helpful. It is drawn from several sources, including choice theory, neuro-linguistic programming (Andreas and Andreas 1989), and the work of Byron Katie (1997).

First, identify your feelings about the other person and the labels you use (for example, pigheaded, narrow minded, spiteful, and condescending). Then ask, "Are these things true?" Is your chosen perception really the way the other person is? Further, ask how you can be certain that your perception is true. As you involve yourself in this sometimes painful inquiry, you realize that it is virtually impossible to know conclusively that your perception represents the truth, even when it is reasonably valid.

The most important step of this process is asking yourself what benefit you receive from maintaining your perception of the other. At this point, you confront the choice theory notion that all behavior—including yours—is purposeful. You discover that you derive some benefit from perceiving the other negatively. As much as you may not like to admit it, you discover that holding that perception is need-satisfying.

Once you have made that discovery, you can begin moving from anger to calm acceptance. First, you acknowledge that whatever you get from your negative emotions is important. Next, you determine how you can get that same benefit without resorting to the kind of negative thoughts, feelings, and behaviors that prevent you from being the kind of person you want to be. When you reach this point, the negativity dissipates. It has served its purpose, assisting you until you were able to come up with a more effective alternative. Far from reflecting weakness, this process allows you to remain in effective control of your life regardless of the behaviors of those around you.

SUMMARY

Conflict will be a part of any long-term relationship. Managed well, it leads to growth. Inspiring teachers value, rather than fear, conflict. They do not seek to avoid or eliminate it, because they know that when conflict is driven underground, it becomes nearly impossible to manage successfully. Instead, inspiring teachers view conflict as a reflection that all are comfortable enough to make known what they want. Understanding that conflict offers an opportunity to achieve even more quality in their lives, they approach the conflict-management process openly, honestly, passionately, energetically, and respectfully. They strive for the ideal of a win/win outcome. Finally, when reaching a win/win outcome is not possible, inspiring teachers remain calm, centered, and focused regardless of how those around them behave. They respectfully work toward negotiating an outcome that is acceptable to everyone.

CHAPTER 9

Time Management

Becoming an inspiring teacher takes considerable effort. Not content to use the same lessons year after year, inspiring teachers continually update and change their learning plans. Because this effort takes time, inspiring teachers need to acquire time-management skills. Otherwise, they risk suffering burnout from stress and overwork. Unfortunately, one coping strategy some teachers consider is returning to a less demanding teaching style. While withdrawing may help them survive, it does not allow them to become, or remain, inspiring teachers.

Teachers who implement many of the strategies in this book find that their jobs actually become more manageable. One reason is that responsibility is appropriately shifted more toward students. When teachers take time to discuss their job and the students' job with students (see chapter 5) and regularly refer to the roles everyone in the class has developed and endorsed, they find there is more time spent on important tasks and less on peripheral, nonessential tasks. In general, teachers are busy, but they are not necessarily busy doing what is most important. Inspiring teachers routinely ask, "Is the task I am engaged in the most appropriate for me given my role and mission in this system?" Some tasks that many traditional teachers spend considerable time doing are not necessarily worth the effort.

Inspiring teachers decide where and how they will invest their time and energy. They take control of their professional lives by acting professionally. Of course, they don't make these important decisions in a vacuum. Before acting, they carefully consider their professional roles and responsibilities, codes of ethical conduct, and school district policy. With these important concerns in mind, inspiring teachers are able to identify areas where they have spent too much unproductive time, freeing them to do the more important work that has the potential to inspire quality and make teaching the joyful experience it should be.

STUDENT EVALUATION

Student evaluation is one area where many traditional teachers spend too much time. Inspiring teachers explain the importance of self-evaluation to students and then provide them with the skills to evaluate themselves in a meaningful, productive way. As a result, teachers avoid much unnecessary correcting, and students begin taking more responsibility for improving their work before getting teacher feedback. If teachers work only in this area, they will save countless hours while providing their students with an important skill that will serve them well throughout their lives.

Teaching students how to evaluate themselves in an academic setting takes time, but it is an investment that pays enormous dividends. Inspiring teachers engage students in the process of developing meaningful rubrics. They analyze models of quality work with students. By intentionally structuring the self-evaluation process, inspiring teachers help students make useful decisions about the quality of their work and improve their efforts without unnecessary teacher intervention. Students who have been taught how to self-evaluate effectively become more responsible, independent learners. Teachers working with these students have more time to do the things that make teaching enjoyable.

DON'T GRADE EVERYTHING

Grading papers was one of my most time-consuming tasks when I taught seventh-, eighth-, and ninth-grade English. The task was made more onerous because I strongly believed that much of my work was done for no real purpose. After I spent hours correcting a set of papers, too many of my students barely looked at my comments. My hard work was largely for naught. I have since learned from other teachers that my experience was typical.

During my last two years in the classroom, my school district focused on student writing. The English department developed guidelines that required students to do a certain amount of writing every week. What had been a daunting task quickly became overwhelming. Sometimes our most creative and effective behaviors are born in desperate times. This was one of those occasions.

Having decided that it was impossible to read and correct each piece of student writing, I developed a folder system (portfolios were not yet a common practice). Students put each writing assignment into their folders after it had been edited. At various points, I told the students that I would be evaluating papers. I might say: "Each of you should now have six papers in your folder. You have completed three descriptive pieces and three persuasive pieces. Choose one paper that you want to make sure I evaluate. I will be certain to look at that one. I will then randomly choose two more pieces, one persuasive and one descriptive. Make sure that anything you have put in your folder represents your best work and that you are ready to have me look at it. All six papers should be in the folder when I collect it next week."

When I switched to this system, several things happened. First, because the students knew that anything in their folders might be assessed, they began taking their assignments more seriously. I stopped hearing, "Is this going to count?" Second, because the students knew I would make sure all of their assignments were completed, they didn't mind that I read only selected pieces. They wanted credit for work they had done, but they didn't need comments on every piece.

Third, because students selected one paper they wanted me to read and evaluate, they more carefully evaluated their work. They reviewed their papers and decided what represented their best work. Since I always reviewed their best work, they believed the system was fair. Giving them a choice also addressed most adolescents' strong need for freedom.

I had very few complaints from students when I routinely used this folder system. If students thought that they had been "unlucky" because I had read some of their poorer samples, I was willing to read more. The amount of reading and correcting I had to do, however, dropped significantly. I had more time to develop interesting, creative, and useful learning plans for the students, and I enjoyed my last two years in the classroom even more.

STUDENT-CENTERED CLASSROOMS

By creating student-centered classrooms, teachers can save valuable time. This type of classroom is characterized by much more student activity and involvement than the traditional teacher-centered classroom. Inspiring teachers do not spend too much time creating lengthy lectures and teacher-centered "performances" designed to capture the imagination of even the most reluctant learners. Instead, they create an engaging environment that encourages all students to become active, fully involved participants in their own learning.

Brain research suggests students need time to make meaning from what has been presented in class. As students learn, inspiring teachers provide them with ample opportunities to interact with the content and with each other, reflect on their work, and process new information. In this environment, inspiring teachers are free to assist, coach, and, if necessary, provide individual assistance and remediation. They are available to students for all the teachable moments that will regularly occur in inspiring classrooms.

THE TEACHER AS A FACILITATOR

Another way many inspiring teachers better manage their time is by minimizing the role of expert and emphasizing the role of facilitator. Inspiring teachers don't need to know everything. Today, new information is disseminated so rapidly that it is difficult even for experts to stay current. Inspiring teachers' primary goal is to excite students and get them on the road to discovery. Teachers can best do that by pointing students in the direction where information is available. They don't have to be the source of all information.

Many years ago, I was told that if a student asked me a question and I didn't know the answer, I should say, "I don't know the answer, but I'll get back to you as soon as I can with the information." Answering that way keeps the teacher in the position of information provider. It also perpetuates the notion that it is the teacher's job to do all the work. I encourage teachers to respond this way: "That's an interesting question. Do you have any idea where you could find information to help you answer it? If not, maybe I can help you figure out where to look. When you've got some information, I'd be interested in hearing what you've learned. We could even develop a way for you to share what you've learned with the rest of the class if that seems like a good idea."

This approach does several things. First, it acknowledges the curiosity that many students bring to class. Second, it enables students to become the experts and gain a sense of power responsibly in the classroom. Third, it frees the teacher from having to spend time on additional research. Finally, it demonstrates that the teacher is creating a community of learners and is available to help students develop the ability to contribute to the learning of the group.

A LIFE OUTSIDE THE CLASSROOM

The inspiring teacher intentionally works to create a satisfying, well-balanced life. Even the most dedicated teachers cannot inspire if they are unhappy. Over the years, I have seen too many wonderfully dedicated teachers neglect their personal needs for freedom and fun. Their passion for teaching and learning sustained them for a while, but eventually they burned out. They had created lives that were painfully out of balance and ultimately unsatisfying. Devoted almost exclusively to the role of teacher, they forgot that they needed time outside school to relax, have fun, and socialize. Had they developed better time-management skills, they might have become happier—and better—teachers. If you want to become an inspiration to your students, find ways to address your needs appropriately and to manage your time so that you can bring your energy, love of teaching, and happiness to the classroom.

EMPOWERING AND EMPLOYING STUDENTS

In many school systems, teachers are asked to perform tasks that seem incongruent with their training, expertise, and professional stature. They often cite such chores as checking hall passes, signing students in and out of lavatories, and supervising students at lunch as a waste of talent. Ironically, some teachers routinely perform equally nonprofessional tasks in their classrooms.

Inspiring teachers define themselves as professionals. Before voluntarily undertaking any task in their classrooms, they ask, "Is this something that I should be doing, or is this a chore I can appropriately delegate to the students?" To discover which tasks, if any, they can give to students and which ones should appropriately remain in their domain, they ask, "If I provide sufficient training, could the students do this task as well as I can? Will doing this task help the students grow socially or academically, or both? If I turn this task over to the students, will I have more time to be an effective, professional teacher?" Teachers might find, for example, that students can learn how to handle routine clerical tasks. Students usually develop a legitimate sense of power and responsibility in a classroom when their energy is used in doing some of the chores that inspiring teachers gladly relinquish.

EFFECTIVE USE OF PARAPROFESSIONALS

In many schools, paraprofessionals (sometimes called classroom aides) and other support personnel are woefully underused. Inspiring teachers find ways to use paraprofessionals more effectively in an effort to give themselves more time.

Paraprofessionals, like the rest of us, need to feel competent and important. Meaningful work helps satisfy this need for power. It is common for paraprofessionals to be given relatively mundane tasks, even though they frequently have a variety of valuable skills. In many cases, paraprofessionals would welcome the opportunity to contribute more substantially to the educational process. Of course, paraprofessionals should not be asked to do something for which they are unprepared or untrained. They can, however, do more than they often do.

Paraprofessionals can provide tutorial or remedial services to individual students. While some students clearly require the expertise of a special-needs teacher to help them learn effectively, many learners thrive when paraprofessionals give them individualized attention in the regular classroom.

Paraprofessionals can also reduce the teacher's workload by correcting certain assignments. This and other time-consuming clerical tasks can easily be managed by someone other than the teacher. Paraprofessionals and teachers can use computers to assist in many clerical tasks as well. More and more educators are finding that when they have to provide students and parents with information on grades and current progress, computers help save time.

Inspiring teachers work diligently to develop supportive and effective working relationships with paraprofessionals.

Most paraprofessionals who work with more than one teacher will say that they work harder and more enthusiastically for some teachers than for others. Ask them why, and they will use words such as "valued," "respected," and "useful." They appreciate being treated professionally and respectfully. Under those conditions, most paraprofessionals will provide tremendous support to teachers and help make the classroom a more productive learning environment.

SUMMARY

It takes time and energy to become an inspiring teacher. Teachers can, however, use various strategies to manage time more effectively and make the journey easier. When students are taught how to evaluate their own work, they become more independent and responsible learners. Being judicious about assessing student work also helps inspiring teachers manage their time more effectively. By structuring student-centered classrooms where teachers serve as facilitators and students are actively involved in learning, teachers are more available to those students who require extra attention. Finally, inspiring teachers delegate appropriate classroom tasks to paraprofessionals and students. As inspiring teachers discover ways to better manage their time, they free themselves to do the work that makes teaching a joyful experience.

Final Thoughts

I began this book with the statement that teaching is the noblest profession. Perhaps that statement should be amended. It would be more accurate to say that teaching has the potential to be the noblest profession. Whether we achieve that nobility is determined by our willingness to inspire.

Every student deserves to be inspired. Every student deserves the opportunity to work with a passionate, caring, knowledgeable professional who brings the curriculum to life by making it meaningful, enjoyable, and vibrant.

The inspired classroom has a dynamic quality that makes it like no other place on earth. It is the place where children are encouraged to develop into lifelong learners and critical thinkers who will make significant contributions to our world. It is the place where genius is born.

Students are not the only ones who flourish in an inspired classroom. Teachers gain even as they give. Inspiring teachers transform teaching from a job into a noble profession. Inspiring teachers make a difference in the world. Inspiring teachers touch the future.

Every teacher has the capacity to inspire. If you are already traveling the path toward nobility, I wish you continued success. If you are just taking your first steps, the joy you will experience as you make a positive difference in the lives of children will make this sometimes challenging journey an exhilarating experience. Don't settle for anything else. You deserve nothing less.

Bibliography

Biehler, R. 1981. *Child Development: An Introduction.* 2d ed. Boston: Houghton Mifflin.

Boffey, B.1993. *Reinventing Yourself: A Control Theory Approach to Becoming the Person You Want to Be.* Chapel Hill, N.C.: New View Publications.

Buck, N. 1997. "Peaceful Parenting." Ph.D. diss., The Union Institute, Cincinnati.

Building Parent Partnerships. NEA Teacher-to-Teacher Books. 1996. Washington, D.C.: The National Education Association.

Burns, R. C. 1993. *Parents and Schools: From Visitors to Partners.* Washington, D.C.: The National Education Association.

Covey, S. 1989. *The Seven Habits of Highly Effective People.* New York: Simon and Schuster.

Crawford, D., R. Bodine, and R. Hoglund. 1993. *The School for Quality Learning: Managing the School and Classroom the Deming Way.* Champaign, Ill.: Research Press.

Csikszentmihalyi, M. 1990. Flow: *The Psychology of Optimal Experience*. New York: HarperCollins.

Elkind, D. 1970. *Children and Adolescents: Interpretive Essays on Jean Piaget*. New York: Oxford University Press.

—. 1981. *The Hurried Child: Growing Up Too Fast, Too Soon*. Reading, Mass.: Addison-Wesley.

—. 1984. *All Grown Up and No Place to Go: Teenagers in Crisis*. Reading, Mass.: Addison-Wesley.

—. 1987. *Miseducation: Preschoolers at Risk*. New York: Alfred A. Knopf.

Gardner, H. 1993. *Frames of Mind: The Theory of Multiple Intelligences*. New York: BasicBooks.

Gilligan, Carol. 1993. *In a Different Voice: Psychological Theory and Women's Development*. Cambridge, Mass.: Harvard University Press.

Glasser, W. 1990. *The Quality School: Managing Students without Coercion*. New York: HarperCollins.

—. 1993. *The Quality School Teacher*. New York: HarperCollins.

—. 1998. *Choice Theory: A New Psychology of Personal Freedom*. New York: HarperCollins.

Gossen, D., and J. Anderson. 1995. *Creating the Conditions: Leadership for Quality Schools*. Chapel Hill, N.C.: New View Publications.

Greene, B. 1994. *New Paradigms for Creating Quality Schools.* Chapel Hill, N.C.: New View Publications.

Halpern, S. 1985. *Sound Health: The Music and Sounds That Make Us Whole.* San Francisco: Harper and Row.

Howard, P. 1994. *The Owner's Manual for the Brain: Everyday Applications from Mind-Brain Research.* Austin, Tex.: Leornian Press.

How Difficult Can This Be? 1989. Produced and directed by Peter Rosen. 70 min. Peter Rosen Productions and PBS Video. Videocassette.

Jensen, E. 1995. *Brain-Based Learning and Teaching.* Del Mar, Calif.: Turning Point Publishing.

—. 1996. *Completing the Puzzle: The Brain-Based Approach.* Del Mar, Calif.: Turning Point Publishing.

—. 1998. *Teaching with the Brain in Mind.* Alexandria, Va.: Association for Supervision and Curriculum Development.

Johnson, D. W., R. T. Johnson, and E. J. Holubec. 1993. *Circles of Learning: Cooperation in the Classroom.* 4th ed. Edina, Minn.: Interaction Book Co.

Katie, B. 1997. "The Work: The Technology of Freedom." The Center for the Work, Barstow, Calif. Booklet.

Kegan, R. 1982. *The Evolving Self: Problem and Process in Human Development.* Cambridge: Harvard University Press.

Kohn, A. 1993. *Punished by Rewards: The Trouble with Gold Stars, Incentive Plans, A's, Praise, and Other Bribes.* Boston: Houghton Mifflin.

LeDoux, J. 1996. *The Emotional Brain: The Mysterious Underpinnings of Emotional Life*. New York: Simon and Schuster.

Lickona, T. 1983. *Raising Good Children: From Birth through the Teenage Years*. New York: Bantam Books.

Ludwig, S., and K. Mentley. 1997. *Quality is the Key: Stories from Huntington Woods*. Wyoming, Mich.: KWM Educational Services.

Multiple Intelligences. NEA Teacher-to-Teacher Books. 1996. Washington, D.C.: National Education Association

Nunn, R. and J. Gallaher. 1998. *Inspiring Tranquility: Stress Management and Learning Styles in the Inclusive Classroom*. Washington, D.C.: National Education Association.

Peck, M. S. 1988. *The Different Drum: Community-Making and Peace*. New York: Touchstone.

Rogers, S., J. Ludington, and S. Graham. 1997. *Motivation and Learning: A Teacher's Guide to Building Excitement for Learning and Igniting the Drive for Quality*. Evergreen, Colo.: Peak Learning Systems.

Rozanski, A. 1988. "Mental Stress and the Induction of Silent Ischemia in Patients with Coronary Artery Disease." New England Journal of Medicine 318 (16): 1005-12.

Russell, P. 1979. *The Brain Book*. New York: Penguin Books.

Schacter, D. 1996. *Searching for Memory: The Brain, the Mind, and the Past*. New York: BasicBooks.

Shea, J., M. Madden, and A. B. Shea. 1997. "Creating Your Own Homework." Plymouth, Mass. Photocopy.

Sullo, R. 1993. *Teach Them to Be Happy*. Chapel Hill, N.C.: New View Publications.

—. 1997. *Inspiring Quality in Your School: From Theory to Practice*. Washington, D.C.: NEA Professional Library.

Sylwester, R. 1995. *A Celebration of Neurons: An Educator's Guide to the Human Brain*. Alexandria, Va.: Association for Supervision and Curriculum Development.

Time Strategies: Block Scheduling and Beyond. NEA Teacher-to-Teacher Books. 1994. Washington, D.C.: The National Education Association.

Wubbolding, R. 1988. *Using Reality Therapy*. New York: Harper-Collins.

Web Sites

The following Web sites provide rich information and links to other valuable sites.

Inspiring Quality: www.capecod.net/bobsullo

The Quality Schools Forum: www.qualityschools.com

The William Glasser Institute: www.wglasserinst.com

The Brain Store/Brainstorm:
www.thebrainstore.com/brain_storm.html

About the Author

Bob Sullo is a school psychologist with the Plymouth Public Schools in Massachusetts, where he has worked since 1974. A senior faculty member of The William Glasser Institute, he travels across the country providing professional development workshops and other training promoting choice theory, quality schools, and brain-based learning.

If you are interested in workshops, presentations, keynotes, or other presentations by the author, contact Bob Sullo directly at:

PO Box 1336
Sandwich, MA 02563
tel: (508) 888-7627
e-mail: rasullo@capecod.net

For additional information, visit the author's web site: http://www.capecod.net/bobsullo